TECHNIQUES OF THE SAMURAI SWORDSMEN

TOSHISHIRO OBATA

Disclaimer

The publisher of this instructional book WILL NOT BE HELD RESPONSIBLE in any way whatsoever for any physical injury, or damage of any sort, that may occur as a result of reading and/or following the instructions given herein. It is essential therefore, that before attempting any of the physical activities described or depicted in this book, the reader or readers should consult a qualified physician to ascertain whether the reader or readers should engage in the physical activity described or depicted in this book.

As the physical activities described or depicted herein may be overly taxing or sophisticated for the reader or readers, it is *essential that this advice be followed and a physician consulted.*

This high quality educational book is produced by Dragon Books. To facilitate learning, high definition photographs have been used throughout, from which distracting background material has been painstakingly removed by expert artists. Printed on fine paper, the book is sewn to allow it to lay flat for easy study without damaging the binding, and is protected against soiling by a laminated cover.

Published by

dragon books

FURIN KAZAN

The Takeda Samurai

Swift as the Wind
Quiet as the Forest
Fierce as Fire
Immovable as a Mountain

Acknowledgements

Publisher	David Chambers
Translation	Haruko Chambers
Design and Layout	Island Design
U.S. Distributor	Dragon Publishing Corp
Printed and Bound by	Anchor Brendon Ltd
	Tiptree, Essex, England

First Published March 1988

ISBN No. 0 946062 22 6
L.C.C.C. No. 87-70956

The Publisher gratefully acknowledges the assistance of the following persons in the production of this book; Gozo Shioda Sensei and Mr. Takeno for the information on the Yoshinkan school; Frances Seyssel-Hawley for allowing us access to the Hawley Library; Bernie Lau for his generous help with the acquisition of historical photographs and Donald Angier for the photograph of the young Sokaku Takeda. And last but not least, Takashi Horiuchi for assisting the author in the demonstration of the techniques.

CONTENTS

Sokaku Takeda 1860-1943, swordsman and master of Daito Ryu Aikibujutsu. His teachings form the firm foundation upon which all present day aikido is based.

Preface

Furuki o tazune atarashiki o shiru
Study the old to understand the new

Japanese Proverb.

Although many books have been published on the subject of modern Aikido, few if any have before been available on the much older art of Aikijujutsu, from which Aikido was developed. Furthermore, what books there were, tended to deal with only one of the modern styles now being practised in order to promote it, and its own particular philosophy. Unfortunately, many of these modern forms have moved so far from the original teachings of Aikijujutsu that much of their vigour has been lost, and they can therefore no longer be classified as martial arts.

For example, from the fountain head of ancient Aikijujutsu knowledge have flowed three main streams of Aikido. One teaches the principal of spiritual enlightenment through the development of internal power or 'ki'. Yet another presents it as a sport to be used in education and competition, while the third has maintained the art in its original combat effective form.

This book, as well as being a practical training manual, is an attempt to inform the reader of the history of Aikijujutsu, and therefore Aikido, and outline the persons involved in its development to its present level. It is not the voice of any particular style of Aikido, but rather the result of research, both practical and academic, over many years by those who have participated in its production. We hope the reader, whatever form of Aikido he or she may practice, will come to regard it as a useful reference work in their own studies, as well as a source of ideas and inspiration.

The only criticism that we make, and it is a positive one, is that modern Aikido has become remote from its roots, and in some cases completely severed from them, and as a result has lost much of its effectiveness. Students must understand that the art they study was designed solely for conflict, and if this concept is deviated from, the thing itself will have no value. This does not mean that we advocate violence, simply that we recommend the art is used for the purpose for which it was created, the containment and supression of violence.

MINAMOTO NO YOSHIMITSU 1056-1127. Founder of Takeda and Ogasawara schools of Archery, Daito Ryu Aikijujutsu (Takeda Ryu) and Kosyu Ryu Gunpo (Military Strategy).

MINAMOTO NO YOSHIKIYO, founded the Takeda branch of the Minamoto family in the province of Kai.

TAKEDA HARUNOBU (SHINGEN) 1520-1573. Lord of Kai, passed on the art of military strategy known as 'Kosyu Ryu Gunpo'.

TAKEDA KUNITSUGU, established the Takeda family in the province of Aizu.

SANADA YUKITAKA, a retainer of Takeda Shingen and noted for his mastery of the art of 'Senpo' (guerilla tactics).

SANADA MASAYUKI, a master of Senpo and Ninjutsu (espionage).

SANADA YUKIMURA, widely regarded as one of the finest Samurai that ever lived, expert in the use of Ninjutsu. Fought for Toyotomi Hideyoshi at the winter and summer campaigns of Osaka Castle.

SANADA NOBUYUKI, fought against his brother at Osaka with the army of Tokugawa Ieyasu.

YAMAMOTO KANSUKE, a retainer of Takeda Shingen and famous for his knowledge and ability in the area of military strategy. Wrote the ultimate martial arts book, 'Heiho Okugi Sho' around 1580.

OBATA TORAMORI, a retainer of Takeda Shingen, a specialist in Kosyu Ryu military strategy.

OBATA KANBEI KAGENORI, Kosyu Ryu Military Strategy.

From this tradition the following martial arts developed; Hojo Ryu, Yamaga Ryu, Kobayakawa Ryu, Kosyu Ryu Kasaiha, Sanada Ryu, Arisawa Ryu and Tominaga Ryu.

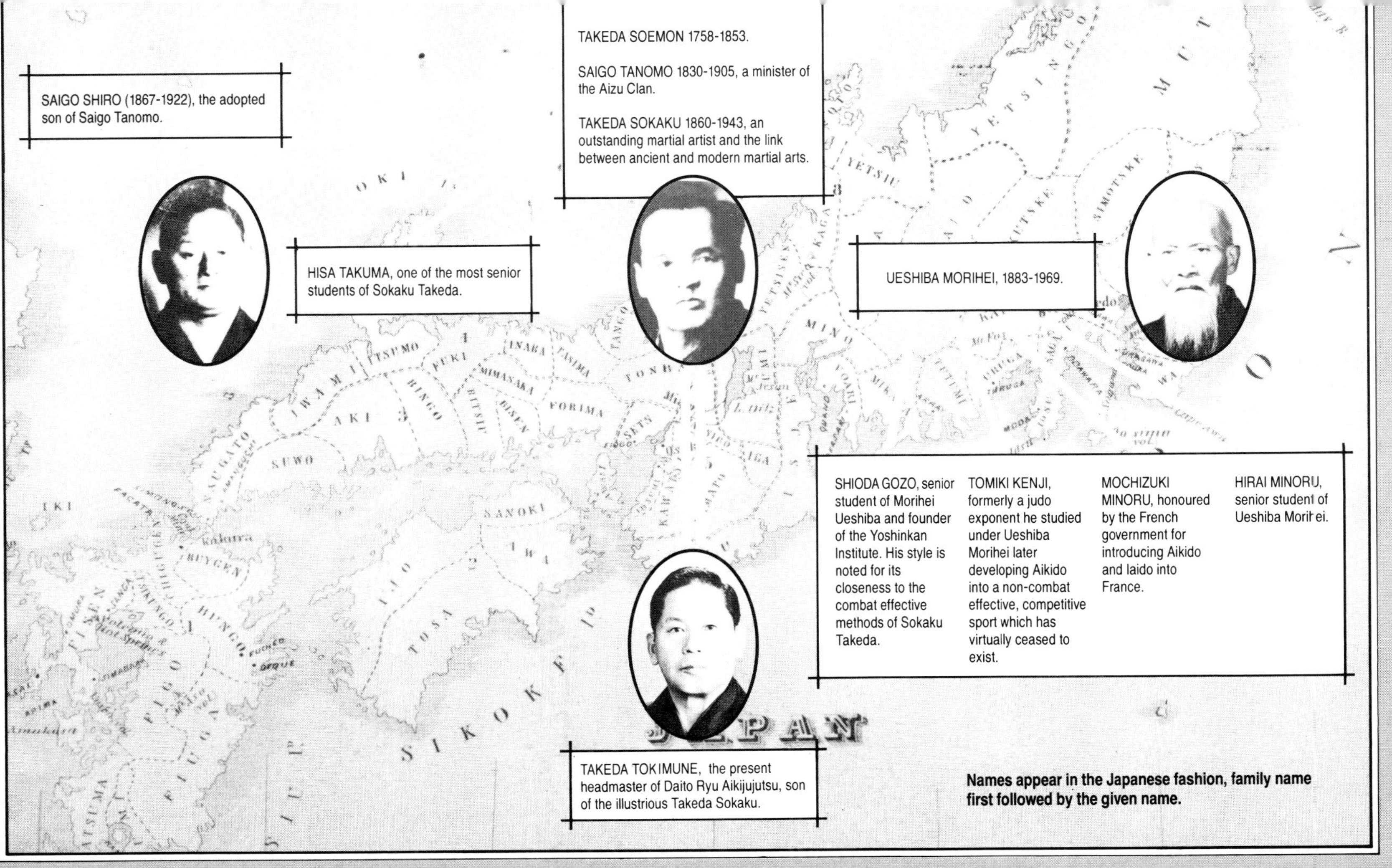

SAIGO SHIRO (1867-1922), the adopted son of Saigo Tanomo.
TAKEDA SOEMON 1758-1853.
SAIGO TANOMO 1830-1905, a minister of the Aizu Clan.
TAKEDA SOKAKU 1860-1943, an outstanding martial artist and the link between ancient and modern martial arts.
HISA TAKUMA, one of the most senior students of Sokaku Takeda.
UESHIBA MORIHEI, 1883-1969.
SHIODA GOZO, senior student of Morihei Ueshiba and founder of the Yoshinkan Institute. His style is noted for its closeness to the combat effective methods of Sokaku Takeda.
TOMIKI KENJI, formerly a judo exponent he studied under Ueshiba Morihei later developing Aikido into a non-combat effective, competitive sport which has virtually ceased to exist.
MOCHIZUKI MINORU, honoured by the French government for introducing Aikido and Iaido into France.
HIRAI MINORU, senior student of Ueshiba Morihei.
TAKEDA TOKIMUNE, the present headmaster of Daito Ryu Aikijujutsu, son of the illustrious Takeda Sokaku.
JAPAN
Names appear in the Japanese fashion, family name first followed by the given name.

Minamoto No Yoshimitsu 1036-1127, credited with the invention of Aikijutsu.

1 Ancient Times

Ancient records inform us that Aikijujutsu was originally developed by Minamoto no Yoshimitsu the third son of Minamoto no Yoriyoshi who was the 5th generation descendant of the Emperor Seiwa. The Minamoto family were one of the major ruling clans of Japan at that time, and one from which many famous fighting men and officials sprang. Although history attributes the foundation of Aikijujutsu to this one individual and his elder brother Yoshiie, more probably it was a fighting method that developed within the clan from the time that they came to prominence, that was perfected by these two brothers.

From actual historical records we know that their father Minamoto no Yoriyoshi, who was ruler of Chinjufu area of Oshu and his eldest son waged war against Abe no Sadatou in the Zen Ku Nen war (1051-1062). The war was long and hard, but victory finally came in September 1062 after the defeat of Abe no Sadatou at the battle of Koromogawa no Yakata.

Twenty years later, the Kiyohara family in the province of Oshu rebelled and the Gosannen war (1083-1087) broke out and was notable for the bitterness of both the weather and the fighting, much of which took place in deep snow. When Yoshiie was heavily engaged and in danger of losing, Yoshimitsu set out to help his brother. When the two forces joined to attack Kanazawa Castle, Yoshimitsu noticed a flight of wild geese overhead that suddenly became disorganised and this alarmed him. He correctly guessed that their enemies were lying in wait for them in accordance with the teachings of the military strategist Ooe no Masafusa, and changed his plans to frustrate those of their enemies. They finally emerged victorious from the war on November 14th 1087.

Minamoto no Yoshiie (Hachimantaro) 1041-1108.

It is said in the old records that the research done by Yoshimitsu and his brother into bone structure and the functioning of the human body, led to the development of Aikijujutsu. Many believe that his research took the form of dissecting cadavres to learn how bones and their related tissues functioned, and from this knowledge techniques were developed. Certainly both heros repeatedly distinguished themselves as great warriors, Minamoto no Hachimantaro Yoshiie as an archer, and Minamoto no Yoshimitsu as a teacher of So-jutsu (spear), To-ho (swordsmanship) and Tai-jutsu (later called Jujutsu), as well as archery.

The eldest son of Yoshimitsu, Yoshikiyo, moved to the area known as Kai and founded a new branch of the family called from that time the "Kaigenjitakeda". Kai the area, Genji the original root name of the family, and Takeda the new family name. The Takeda family developed its own unique forms of martial arts including archery*, horsemanship, spear, sword and Aikijujutsu techniques. They supplemented their positive battlefield methods known collectively as 'heiho', with effective 'gunpo' (field strategy) methods of diverting rivers (to flood the enemies camp or deprive him of his water supply), and tunnel digging (to mine gold or enter the enemy's castle by digging beneath its walls).

**Takeda Ryu and Ogasawara Ryu are the only two schools of mounted archery that exist today. The formal records of both schools give Minamoto no Yoshimitsu as their founder.*

The only remaining schools of mounted archery (yabusame) are the Takeda and Ogasawara methods, both of which give their founder as Minamoto no Yoshimitsu.

The Decline of the Kai Takeda

Towards the end of the Sengoku era, the remarkable and illustrious Takeda family threw up yet another great warrior hero, Takeda Shingen. A great leader of men and a fierce adversary he waged war against Uesugi Kenshin the ruler of the state of Echigo. Their most famous engagement was at Kawanakajima in 1561.

Takeda Shingen owed his enormous success in military matters not only to his own talent and ambition, but also to a remarkable group of retainers, all of whom were notable in their own right. Sanada Yukitaka and his family achieved remarkable results in battle even when fighting on the losing side. Obata Toramori proved himself time and time again a fearless warrior, while Yamamoto Kansuke was a brilliant military planner and strategist*. The combination of their remarkable talents proved for many years an insurmountable obstacle to the military objectives of rival neighbouring states.

In 1572 Takeda Shingen took on the might of Tokugawa Ieyasu and beat him conclusively, only to die soon afterwards of wounds received on the journey to Kyoto at a time and place that history does not record. In April 1573 Takeda Kunitsugu took the last will and testament of Takeda Shingen to their ally Ashina Moriuji the ruler of the state of Aizu. Ashina Moriuji gave him a mansion with much land around it and persuaded him to stay within his fief as a master of swordsmanship. As life for the Kai branch of the Takeda family was becoming difficult in their own area, the offer was readily accepted.

The cavalry of Takeda Shingen's son Katsuyori were the elite fighting troops of the period, and considered by many generals to be invincible. It was with some confidence therefore that 15,000 of them attacked the combined forces of Tokugawa Ieyasu and Oda Nobunaga on May 21st 1575 in a battle that it now known to historians as Nagashino no Kassen. The sight of so many mounted Samurai, armed to the teeth and trained from childhood to kill or be killed in battle must have been thought provoking to say the least.

For their enemies, the spectacle of the Takeda cavalry manoeuvring their magnificent mounts at full speed and in complete unison must have been blood chilling. But Tokugawa Ieyasu and Oda Nobunaga had

**Yamamoto Kansuke set down the teachings of the clan in his book Heiho Okugi Sho, (The Inner Secrets of Military Strategy). This remarkable volume gives instruction in the Takeda arts of swordsmanship, unarmed grappling methods (Torite) halberd (naginata) techniques and gunnery as well as the management of men materials and ordinance. Probably the most fascinating part of the book is the second section, a manual of pure strategy which is as relevant in the context of Japanese corporate planning today, as it was on the battlefields of 16th century Japan.*

武田晴信入道信玄
原大隅守
相木市兵衛
真田弾正
一蘭斎國綱
OBATA TORAMOR

Battle of Kawanakajima in 1561 between the armies of Takeda Harunobu (Shingen) on the left bank, and Uesugi Kagetora (Kenshin) on the right. Famous retainers of the Takeda family present at this battle include: Yamamoto Kansuke (the author of Heiho Okugi Sho), Obata Toramori (marked with a white spot, a distant relative of the author), and Sanada Yukitaka.

never underestimated either the skill or dedication of the Takeda warriors, both realised that they could not be overcome by conventional means. They made their plans and they made them well, yet they were not in accord with the Samurai ethic that valued honour and bravery above all things.

Time after time, as the seemingly irresistable waves of the Takeda cavalry swept down upon their enemies, they were cut down by hails of musket balls from matchlock guns known to the Japanese as Tanegashima*. On that fateful day, 12,000 Samurai, the pride of the province of Kai lost their lives and Takeda Katsuyori, having decisively lost the battle had no choice other than to retreat to his native state. During the return to Kai a major treasure of the Takeda family, a famous helmet called Suwahossho no Kabuto that was made by the armour smith Myochin was lost, which would seem to indicate that the retreat was not an orderly one.

In February 1582 the forces of Oda Nobunaga and Tokugawa Ieyasu attacked Katsuyori on his home ground, and after a futile battle against overwhelming odds, Takeda Katsuyori, the last of the Kai Takeda took his own life in the accepted Samurai method of seppuku. So the secret art of Minamoto no Yoshimitsu that had been passed from generation to generation of Takeda Samurai in Kai province, now passed by means of Takeda Kunitsugu to the Samurai of Aizu. The art thus surviving the branch of the family that founded it.

**Guns were introduced into Japan in 1543 quite innocently by Diego Zeimoto a member of the Portuguese trading party of Fernam Mendez Pinto that arrived at the port of Tanegeshima after which the guns were named. Pinto is one of the first recorded European visitors to Japan. When Pinto departed the island empire five and one half months later skilled Japanese armanent makers had already produced six hundred copies of the matchlocks, also called "Hinawaju" literally fire rope gun. When he returned to Japan in 1556 as the ambassador from the Portuguese Viceroy Don Alonso de Noronha, 300,000 were in existence. Although the gun played a major role in Japanese history both at Nagashino and the battle of Sekigahara which established the Tokugawa shogunate, it never advanced much beyond the matchlock design introduced by the 16th century Portuguese visitors.*

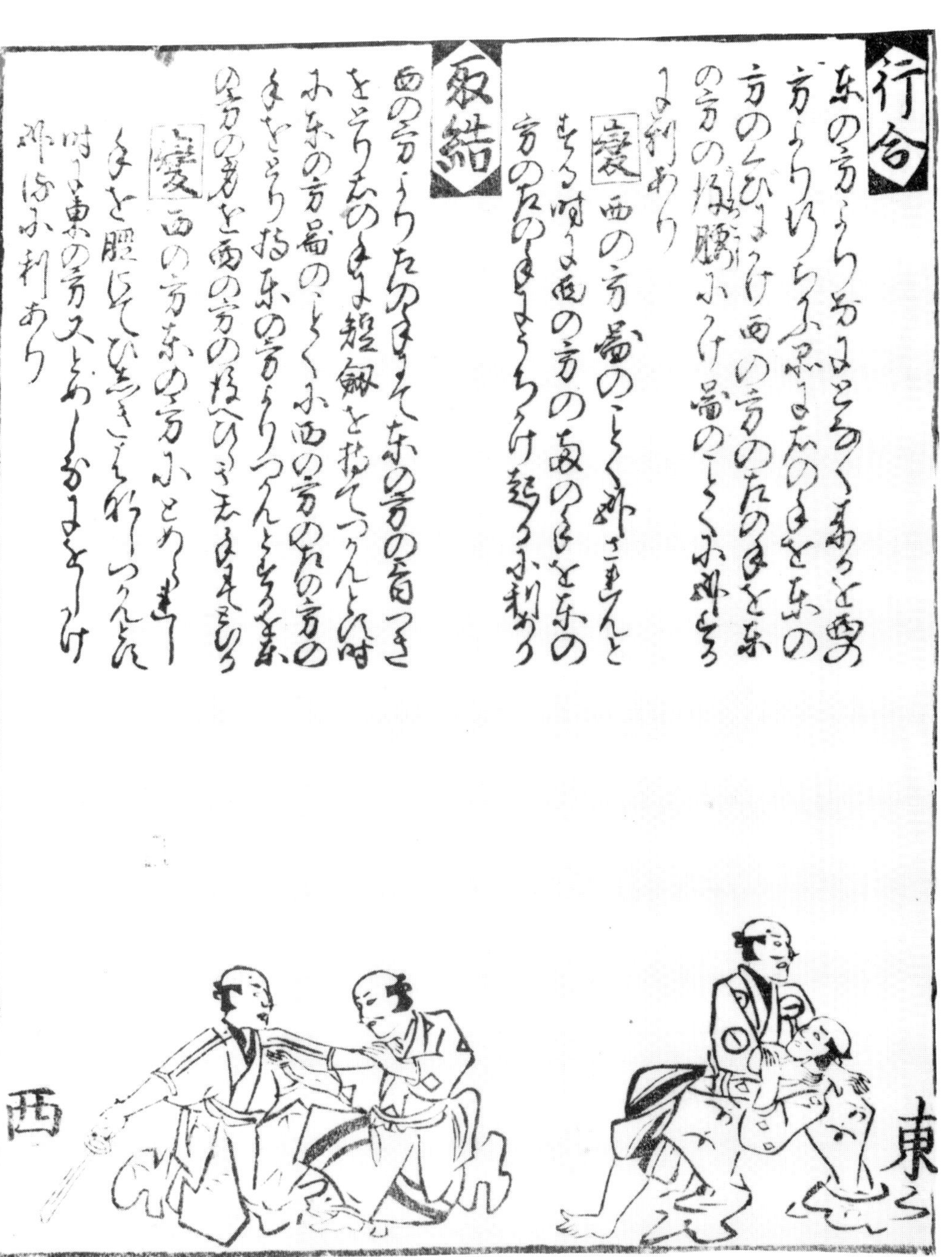

A page from "Heiho Okugi Sho" written around 1580 by Yamamoto Kansuke, a retainer of Takeda Shingen. This shows ancient jujutsu methods involving joint locking and evasive movements similar to the modern Ikajyo, Nikajyo and Irimi-nage techniques. A translation from this ancient manuscript which includes reproductions of much of the original material is published by Dragon Books.

2 The Men of Aizu

Daito Ryu Aikijujutsu (also known Takeda Ryu Aikijujutsu because it was handed down through the Takeda family), was transmitted to the upper echelons of the Aizu Samurai Clan by Takeda Kunitsugu. This branch of the Takeda family which was known not surprisingly as the Aizu Takeda, also taught swordsmanship to the Aizu retainers for many generations. At that time education, both of the body and the mind was considered essential for Samurai youth. Skill at arms was important of course, but so was understanding the Samurai's moral code, therefore schools were set up to provide suitable tuition for young men of the Samurai caste. The Aizu clan school established in 1664 was called the 'Nisshinkan'. The training hall that housed it was erected in 1674.

The martial arts flowered in the Aizu area as they did nowhere else. At the Nisshinkan five styles of swordsmanship were taught as well as two styles of Jujutsu, Mizu no Shinto Ryu and Shinmyo Ryu. Additionally there were many private training halls in the Aizu area including twenty two for Kenjutsu (swordsmanship the training for which was conducted with wooden or bamboo practice swords). Fourteen for batto-jutsu (swordsmanship practised with real swords), sixteen for jujutsu, seven for archery, sixteen for gunnery and four devoted to training with the spear. Would be students could also study Naginata (halberd), Kusari-jutsu (chain methods), and Bojutsu (wooden staff methods), Kacchu Kumiuchi (unarmed grappling in armour) and Jinchyu Ninjutsu (techniques of espionage). In all ninety four martial arts schools thrived in the Aizu area.

Certain martial arts were available only for the very top level of Samurai and were designated "Otome Ryu" (Goshikiuchi) or secret teachings. Knowledge of these methods was not allowed to pass to lower level retainers, nor were technical exchanges between styles allowed, or demonstrations before non-members of the "ryuha" or school. Aiki-jujutsu and Aizu Mizoguchi Ha Itto Ryu were two martial arts covered by these regulations.

The martial methods of the Aizu Samurai were passed from generation to generation, constantly being polished and perfected. After being handed from father to son for ten generations of Aizu Takeda Samurai, they were in the course of time passed on to a group of very remarkable men. This small but very talented group would protect the art they treasured from the political storms that accompanied Japan's emergence into the outside world of the late 19th century, forces that destroyed many of Japan's oldest and most respected martial traditions.

The Time of the Sword is Over

After more than two centuries of rule by the Tokugawa Shogunate during which the country hardly changed at all, Japan was slowly being dragged, often against its will, into the latter part of the nineteenth century. The forces of progress were beginning to exert pressures that neither the Samurai nor the government that controlled them could resist. Finally civil war between the supporters of the Shogun and those that wanted to restore the Emperor to the throne broke out, and a period of bloody civil war ensued, the like of which had not been seen since the time of the Sengoku disturbances three centuries before.

The support for either party, Emperor or Shogun was organised along clan lines. The Aizu Samurai under Katamori Matsudaira, having served the Shogun for centuries continued to serve him still and fought as key troops of the Shogun during the "Bakumatsu" wars (1853-1867). The Emperor supported the Satsuma and Choshu clans at the battles of Toba and Fushimi in January 1868, following which the last Shogun, Yoshinobu Tokugawa escaped from Osaka and fled to Edo, only to relinquish his power and his castle shortly afterwards to the new ruler of the islands of Japan.

In charge of the Aizu Samurai that supported the Shogun at Fushimi was Tanomo Saigo (1830-1905), a student of Soemon Takeda, and an expert in Daito Ryu Aikijujutsu. In the Autumn of 1868, Tanomo Saigo led the Aizu Clan against the combined forces of Satsuma and Choshu at Shirakawaguchi, and after a fierce and bloody battle, was defeated. Yet so noble were they in battle and so true to the finest ethics of the Samurai in defeat, that the name of the Aizu clan will live forever in the hearts of the Japanese people, their names endure as if carved in stone.

When the family of Tanomo Saigo heard that their troops had lost the battle, they assumed that Tanomo Saigo was dead and knew where their duty lay. Realising that they would soon face the hostile troops that had overcome their own warriors, to avoid disgrace and bad treatment at their hands, and so they would not be an encumbrance to the fighters that would defend the homeland, twenty one women and children committed suicide.

Resistance was felt by the Satsuma troops invading the Aizu homeland. A band of Samurai women led by Takeko Nakamura fought tooth and nail with halberds against the invaders, as did the Byakko Tai, a group of

40 young boys between the ages of 15 and 17. When this group of youths eventually lost their leader, they took up position on Mount Iimori and seeing Aizu city in flames, the remaining 20 members of the squad killed themselves to maintain the honour of their families. But as is so often the case the brave and the just are revenged.

In the tenth year of the reign of the Emperor Meiji, the Satsuma troops that had caused the downfall of the Aizu Clan revolted against the Emperor's rule and the Seinan War broke out. When the Aizu Clan was beaten at Shirakawaguchi, many Samurai and commoners from the Aizu area joined the Emperor's police force or army, and it was they that now faced the rebellious Satsuma troops. With the memory of their losses still fresh in their minds, and the spiritual inspiration of the boys troop and the women led by Takeko Nakamura burning in their breasts, they fought like demons and at Tabaruzaka earned a revenge that must have satisfied their dead ancestors, and that sent what remained of the once powerful Satsuma clan into oblivion.

Tanomo Saigo survived the battle at Shirakawaguchi and later would play a decisive part in the passage of Daito Ryu Aikijujutsu into modern times.

3

Sokaku Takeda
1860 – 1943

Sokaku Takeda was born in Aizu Province on October 10th 1860. He learned Jujutsu from his grandfather Soemon Takeda and Bojutsu from his father who was a noted sumo wrestler and champion of the Aizu Clan. In his youth he studied Ono Ha Itto Ryu swordsmanship under Toma Shibuya in Tokyo, and Jikishinkage Ryu from Kenkichi Sakakibara*. In 1876 he received a Menkyo Kaiden (Certificate of graduation) in Ono Ha Itto Ryu.

In June of this year his elder brother died, and family duties took him back to his native Aizu province. On his return he met Tanomo Saigo the minister of the Aizu clan, who had been a student of Sokaku's grandfather Soemon Takeda, and who was also a swordsman in the Mizoguchi Ha Itto Ryu and Koshu Ryu Gungaku traditions. From Tanomo Saigo he learned Aikibujutsu which included spear, sword and other weapons, and from what we can gather, was a brilliant student. It is important to realise that Daito Ryu Aikibujutsu was a complete fighting system that included nage waza (throwing techniques) osae waza (control techniques) batto-jutsu (drawing and striking with the sword), yari justu (use of the spear), and Torae waza (capture techniques). What we currently term jujutsu would have been simply part of the complete fighting system that was used at close quarters, with or without weapons.

In 1880 the two men met again when Tanomo Saigo was a senior priest at Nikko Toshogu and Futarasan Shrines in Tochigi prefecture*. In the six months that they spent together, Tanomo Saigo passed onto his brilliant student all the teachings, including the secret ones of Daito Ryu Aikibujutsu.

From 1880 until 1898, Sokaku Takeda travelled the length and breadth of Japan engaging in contests with every prominent martial arts master that would respond to his challenge. He asked no favours or special consideration from men that were considered his superiors. In fact he handicapped himself by fighting only with his opponent's favourite weapon, so if he faced a master of the spear, he would use a spear, against a famous swordsman he would use a sword. He never lost an

**Toma Shibuya was a famous and very expert swordsman, his adopted son was a classmate of Hakudo Nakayama who is now widely regarded as the father of modern Kendo and Iaido. Kenkichi Sakakibara is known as the last of the Meiji period swordsmen, and became famous for successfully cutting a helmet made by the armour smith Myochin, when all the others had failed.*

**This shrine was established on the death of Tokugawa Ieyasu when he was exhalted to the status of a god. As the Aizu clan had served the Tokugawa Shoguns for centuries it was natural that Katamori Matsudaira and Tanomo Saigo should serve as principal and assistant principal even after the return of power to the Emperor.*

Left: A rare photograph of Sokaku Takeda as a young man. Circa 1888.

engagement and despite the fact that he was constantly on the move, and had no permanent training hall, his students numbered in the region of 30,000 and included Dukes, government ministers, former Daimyos (provincial Samurai Lords) and high ranking officials.

Sokaku Takeda was a member of the last generation of Samurai, a brilliant martial arts master and talented teacher who acquired his skills through devotion and sacrifice from a very young age. What he learnt from his instructors in the training hall, the academic knowledge of techniques and movement, he then perfected in actual combat against men considered his seniors that was unrestricted by regulations or the fear of 'official' interference. These were not 'friendly' competitions by any means, and deaths were not uncommon. Several stories have been handed down through the intervening years that give us an insight into both the man's character and his practical ability.

In 1910 a rural area through which Sokaku Takeda frequently travelled was being terrorised by an audacious robber who was so active and successful, that all but the strongest feared to travel after dark. The Police, despite strenuous efforts had failed to bring his career to an end. Suddenly and for no apparent reason, the felonious activity stopped. Investigations by the Police resulted in the discovery of the robber's dead body, deeply embedded head first in the mud of a rice field close to the route that Sokaku Takeda habitually travelled.

The villagers did not question their good luck, it was assumed that the Aikijujutsu master had thrown the felon into the mud with such force, that he had not been able to escape the clutches of the sodden ground, and had suffocated. On the other hand, it may have been a broken neck resulting from the impact that killed him. Doubtless the villagers and the Police were quite happy with the outcome, and did not therefore investigate the actual cause of death too vigourously.

Five years later he was involved in a brawl with fifty construction workers yet emerged unscathed after inflicting much damage on a numerically superior enemy. At that time many road repairers and building workers were drawn from the ranks of unsuccessful criminals, or former gang members. They were violent, aggressive and usually without a fixed home, wandering here and there with the work, and passing their free time in drinking and fighting. They were such a problem to the Police that if one died as a result of injuries sustained in a brawl, to save time and the trouble of a formal enquiry, he would simply be entered on the official records as having died from natural causes.

Left: Sokaku Takeda's ability was greatly admired by the Police and Military, and throughout his life he was much in demand as a teacher of their officers and men. He is pictured here with a group of Policemen, (fifth from the left.) Circa 1898.

When the fight broke out, despite deing outnumbered fifty to one by desperados armed with tobiguchi (a metal hook on the end of a long pole), iron bars and spear points, he threw several of his assailants. However, when swords were drawn, he armed himself in a similar fashion, and cut down and killed nine of his attackers. This demonstrates the flexibility and strength of a complete fighting system such as Aikibujutsu over a single martial art. Being able to switch without hesitation from unarmed to armed defense, allowed him to emerge victorious from the engagement, despite seemingly impossible odds.

Sokaku Takeda would undoubtedly be regarded as eccentric were he alive today, as it is said that he even carried his own tea making utensils with him to eliminate the possibilty of poisoning, and would eat only food prepared by himself or a senior student*. It seems his appearance also was somewhat bizarre, as the following incident demonstrates. In 1904, Charles Parry an American teacher of English at the Daini Koko a college in Sendai, complained to the ticket inspector on a train in which he was travelling about a fellow passenger of unkempt appearance, who was occupying a first class seat he did not seem capable of paying for. Appropriate questioning, while proving that the passenger did in fact have the highest class of ticket available, enraged him to such an extent that he demanded to know who had complained. On learning that it was the large foreigner in the carriage, the tiny Takeda only 150cm (4′11″) tall and 52kg (114lb.) in weight, grasped Parry with both hands (yonkajyo technique) and led him to the open deck at the rear of the train.

What happened there we shall never know, what is sure is that it had a profound effect on the unfortunate Mr. Parry. He reported to the authorities in the United States that Daito Ryu Aikijujutsu was a superior method of combat and this led to an invitation from President Roosvelt for an instructor to be sent to the United States to demonstrate these strange but effective movements. Accordingly, Sokaku Takeda despatched Shinzo Harada from the Sendai Police Dept, and one of his first students on reaching the United States was Charles Parry the former victim of his own illustrious teacher.

Sokaku Takeda is the link between our time and that of the Samurai, it is he who was responsible for passing on the true way of Aikijujutsu through his students to future generations. There were others as we shall see that paralleled him in time and whose talent approached his

**In years gone by this was considered a legitimate ploy by which a Samurai could protect himself from assassination.*

own, but none would better his achievements, or leave a stronger foundation upon which to build.

After leading a full, successful and what must have been a very exciting life, Sokaku Takeda's natural span of years came to an end on April 25th 1943. He had suffered some paralysis two years before and many had at that time believed his end was very near. It is said that so close was he to death that one of his senior students Morihei Ueshiba, changed the name of his own school from Aikibudo to Aikido, a breach of etiquette to say the least, presumably because he felt his teacher did not have long to live and he could therfore make the change without fear of complaint. However, Sokaku recovered some of his former powers, and despite the paralysis, even threw a Judo sixth dan two months before his death while teaching at Muroran Police Department. On the day that he was taken, he collapsed at Aomori Station at the northerly tip of Japan's main island of Honshu, and was carried to the Ito Hotel by his students, but was found to be dead on arrival. One of the most distinguished fighting men from the last generation of Samurai left this world at the age of eighty three, and it now depended on his students to carry on his work. They were Tokimune Takeda, Yukiyoshi Sagawa, Takuma Hisa, Toyosaku Matsuda, Kakuyoshi Yamamoto and Morihei Ueshiba. Sokaku Takeda had been told by his teacher Tanomo Saigo that the time of the sword was over, and that aikijujutsu was the part of their fighting system that should be given priority. This in turn he had passed on to his students.

Right: Sokaku Takeda was active until the time of his death, and as can be seen from this photograph, retained much of his strength despite his advanced age.

Osaka 1939, Sokaku Takeda with his son Tokimune Takeda (centre) and senior student Takuma Hisa (right).

4

Shiro Saigo

1867 – 1922

Another of Tanomo Saigo's most brilliant pupils was Shiro Shida, a man of great natural talent who at one time was the heir apparent to both the Daito Ryu Aikijujutsu (as Takeda Ryu Aikijujutsu became known) and the Kodokan Judo tradition. Adopted by Tanomo Saigo in 1882 he became Shiro Saigo, the name by which the world would know him*. Tanomo Saigo adopted Shiro Saigo to groom him as his successor, the son that would continue the tradition of Daito Ryu Aikijujutsu. However, Shiro was recruited by Jigoro Kano to head his new "Kodokan" judo movement, therefore Tanomo Saigo also passed on his secrets to the somewhat eccentric Sokaku Takeda who in the full course of time proved to be a most worthy successor.

At the age of fourteen Shiro travelled to Tokyo in the hope of becoming a soldier, but fell short of the minimum required height and was refused. He therefore concentrated anew on his training in jujutsu and rapidly built such a reputation for himself that he came to the attention of Jigoro Kano, the noted reformist educator. Professor Kano, a student of Tenshin Shin yo Ryu*, Kito Ryu and Seki Guchi Ryu Jujutsu, was developing his own style of unarmed method which he called "Judo" from these older styles. He placed great emphasis on its use in education and as a way of building 'character'. He was however making little headway as his style had many deficiencies and was no match for the schools of genuine combat effective jujutsu then in existence. In Shiro Saigo he found the perfect champion for his new movement.

Trained in Daito Ryu Aikijujutsu by Tanomo Saigo, at that time one of the foremost experts in Japan, he had natural ability, great strength and a desire for knowledge. By the time he reached twenty one, he had become fifth dan, the highest award the Kodokan had to offer. In contests against other schools of Jujutsu, he decimated his opponents with the Daito Ryu technique 'Yama Arashi' or mountain storm, a throw with which his name became synonymous. No one else of his generation could master this technique which consisted of a wrist lock combined with a throw, and so deadly was it that most opponents did not rise to their feet for some time after being thrown.

**He would be immortalised in print as Sanshiro Sugata, the Judo champion hero of a novel that appeared some time later, and which helped establish and popularise the judo movement of Jigoro Kano with which at that time he was associated. This novel was actually written by the grandson of Tsunejiro Tomita, one of Professor Kano's most senior students.*

**Tenshin Shin yo Ryu Jujutsu was practised mainly by "Ashigaru", the lowest level of foot soldier in fuedal times, and "Chugen" a sort of man-of-all-work to Samurai. As such it depended on strong hips and a powerful body rather than skill and finesse and was not a match for the methods employed by the Samurai. Modern judo clearly demonstrates, and has indeed exaggerated this dependance on brute strength.*

A MEETING OF JUDO AND JUJUTSU TEACHERS

Front Row Left to Right:
Masamitsu Inazu-Miura Ryu:Yazo Eguchi-Kyushin Ryu:Takayoshi Katayama-Yoshin Ryu:Kumon Hoshino-Shiten Ryu:Jigoro Kano-Kodokan (Judo):Hidemi Totsuka-Yoshin Ryu:Jushin Sekiguchi-Sekiguchi Ryu:Hirotsugu Yano-Takeuchi Santo Ryu:Katsuta Hiratsuka-Yoshin Ryu.

A meeting of Judo and Jujutsu teachers held at the Butokukai Martial Arts Academy in Kyoto Japan on July 24th 1906. The meeting was called to formalise the 'kata' or formal exercises of Judo, and was held in an atmosphere of intense rivalry and mis-trust between the older schools of Jujutsu and the emerging Kodokan Judo movement.

The names of those who attended this historic meeting are as follows:– Teacher's name first followed by his school or method.

Back Row Left to Right:
Kihei Aoyagi-Sosuishitsu Ryu:Mokichi Tusui-Sekiguchi Ryu:-Hirozaburo Oshima-Takeuchi Ryu:Hoken Sato-Kodokan:Ikutaro Imai-Takeuchi Ryu:Mataemon Tanabe-Fusen Ryu:Shikataro Takeno-Takeuchi Ryu:Shuichi Nagaoka-Kodokan:Sakugiro Yokoyama-Kodokan:Hajime Isogai-Kodokan:Yoshiaki Yamshita-Kodokan:

Names are given in the European Fashion,
i.e. given name first followed by family name.

Jigoro Kano intelligently, if a little unfairly, used a master Daito Ryu technician to prove the supremacy of his own judo method, although most of the techniques that Shiro overcame opponents with were not included in the Kano school. In fact, most wrist locks, strikes, strangles and kicks had not been included in the new art because they were considered too dangerous and possibly damaging to young people learning the new Judo in school. By 1905 the Kodokan was teaching 150 or so 'tricks' as they were called, whereas the Daito Ryu repertoire numbered something in excess of 2,000 'waza' or techniques. The Kodokan had also introduced rules for competitions that while limiting the number of injuries, would accelerate the decline of Judo from martial art, (bujutsu) to martial study, (budo) then finally to sport and public spectacle.

The Kodokan was so successful, particularly after the publication of the story based on the life of Shiro Saigo was published, that it even came to the attention of foreigners. By 1905 several books had been published in English on the subject of Mr. Kano's 'jiujitsu' as he was still calling it. The Kodokan's official line was that the older styles of 'jujutsu' were less effective than the new Kano method. They stated publicly that; "Japanese who have learned the old and now obsolete methods have found themselves compelled to forget their hard-acquired knowledge and take instruction all over again in the more scientific Kano method. An adept of the first rank in the older schools finds himself helpless before an ordinarily clever student of Kano"*. They did not mention of course that this only applied if the exponent of jujutsu was unarmed, prohibited from using some of his most effective techniques, eg. strikes, wrist locks, kicks and nerve holds. And even then, the result of a contest would not have been a foregone conclusion.

If Professor Kano's style was so superior, why was he himself using one of the most talented Daito Ryu Aikijujutsu exponents of the age to bring his own school to prominence. Kano knew that the majority of old schools of Jujutsu would not break with tradition and openly teach their methods to all and sundry, so he could challenge them with impunity, secure in the knowledge that few would respond, and those that did would have to contend with the Daito Ryu techniques of Shiro Saigo.

In any case, many of the so called old schools of Jujutsu, "Koryu" as they are called, were not old at all but were comprised of groups of commoners who have taken up the art after the demise of the Samurai class a few decades before. Although many had been taught by Samurai

**The Complete Kano Jiu-Jiutsu by Hancock and Higashi first published by G.P. Putnam and Sons in 1905. Re-published and currently available from Dover Publications Inc. New York.*

trying to eke out a living in the difficult times following the Meiji Restoration, they were for the most part mere diletanti having had no combat experience or training with weapons.

Yet it would be a mistake to be too critical of Professor Kano for he achieved much as an educator, and did manage to have his unified and highly organised school of Judo accepted as the standard method for the Japanese Police Force and Army. At this time Judo retained a few combat effective techniques, effective that is against untrained and unarmed assailants that were dressed in clothes the 'judoka' could take hold in order to perform the Judo technique. Against an armed and well trained Samurai, the new techniques would have been of little practical use.

Shiro Saigo eventually left the ranks of the Kodokan and moved to southern Japan where he worked as a reporter.* One version of the facts has it that pressure from both sides Daito Ryu and Kodokan for his services was so great that he abandoned both. Another, probably more factual account is that while Kano was away in Europe and Shiro therefore in charge, he and several other Jujutsu men got into a fight with some sumo wrestlers. The police were called and arrived in force to try and quieten things down and restore the peace.

Unfortunately several of these courageous officers were thrown into the Sumida River by Shiro Saigo's group as they attempted to negotiate a settlement to the dispute. As Professor Kano was the head of the police Judo organisation serious repercussions were bound to follow, and therefore to avoid them and presumably to save Professor Kano from as much embarassment as possible, he absented himself permanently.

The departure of Shiro Saigo from the Kodokan signified the severance of its connection with the authentic martial arts, from this point Judo lost much of its vitality. In the years that followed, Judo evolved more and more into a sport although its originator had never intended this to be so, and 'hard' judo only really remained in the police and the military. The second world war punctuated the change from semi-effective fighting method (budo form) into a simple sport that has little or no effectiveness in actual combat conditions, and in which the decisive factor is usually brute force and cunning manipulation of the contest rules.

**He eventually became a ninth dan 'hanshi' in kyudo the Japanese form of archery, and died on December 23rd 1922 at the age of 57 years.*

A Judo club in Tokyo around the turn of the century. While the younger students are practising techniques that are similar to modern Judo, the older students (centre left) are practising striking techniques or 'atemi waza' that no longer form part of the Judo repertoire.

5 Morihei Ueshiba and the Aikikai

Morihei Ueshiba was born on December 14th 1883 in the Motomachi district of Tanabe City in Wakayama Prefecture. From an early age he was strongly attracted to, some might say obsessed with religion, and was encouraged by his parents to take up more physical pursuits such as sumo and swimming to counteract this tendency. As a young man he moved to Tokyo and opened a small business, and during the time that he spent in the nation's capital, he studied Kito Ryu Jujutsu and Shinkage Ryu swordsmanship. He returned to his home as a result of ill health, but later around 1903, enlisted in the military and served with some distinction in the Russian Japanese war.

In 1912 Morihei Ueshiba moved to Hokkaido. Japan's most northerly island was being settled with govenment backing to ensure its retention as part of the Japanese Empire. Its strategic position made this essential, especially as the Russians were showing interest in it. Seven years previously with the connivance of the English, Japan had given Russia a mauling that it would not soon forget, so it was essential that the advantage that had been gained was kept, and that meant populating Hokkaido with Japanese citizens as soon as possible.

While he was pioneering in Hokkaido, Ueshiba was introduced to Sokaku Takeda by Kotaro Yoshida, and became a student. For the next seven years he studied under the master while Sokaku Takeda was at the peak of his ability, and in the prime of life. In 1922 at the age of 39, together with only twenty two other people, he was granted the position of 'Kyoju Dairi'*. However two students received higher honours. Yukiyoshi Sagawa and Takuma Hisa both received 'kaiden' and Yukiyoshi also received 'soden' or all techniques, (2,884 waza including staff, sword, two swords, spear, baton, iron fan, missile throwing and short sword methods). Yukiyoshi became the 36th head master of Daito Ryu Aikijujutsu on the death of his teacher, but relinquished his position to his teacher's son, Tokimune Takeda on the latter's safe return from the last war. In 1936 Morihei Ueshiba opened his own school in Tokyo and called his style Aikibudo.

Although he was criticised for changing the name of his 'dojo' so soon after the near fatal attack his teacher suffered in 1941, this may have been a coincidence. In fact he did not seem to be able to settle for any name at first, and called his school at first Ueshiba Juku Aikijujutsu, then Aikibujutsu, followed by Kobukai Aikibudo, Tenshin Aikibudo, Takemusu Aiki and finally Aikido. This name was first registered by

**This signified mastery of the majority of the Daito Ryu techniques. 118 Basic techniques, aikijujutsu okugi 80 techniques, hiden okugi 66 techniques and goshin yo no te 84 techniques.*

Morihei Ueshiba, a student of Sokaku Takeda who developed from Daito Ryu Aikijutsu the modern form known as 'Aikido'.

植芝盛平

教授代理

門人ヲ取リ大東流合氣柔術教授スル場合ハ克
ク其ノ人ノ品行方正ナルヲ選ミテ教授スル事
一門人ニ教授スル場合ハ英名録ニ住所氏名年齢
并ニ道場ノ地名教授日數ヲ記載シ之ニ捺印セ
シムル事
一門人ニ教授スル場合ハ豫メ入門料トシテ一人ニ付
金參圓宛武田大先生ニ納入スル事

大正拾壹年九月拾五日

Above: 1916, Morihei Ueshiba as a student of Daito Ryu Aikijutsu under Sokaku Takeda. The document (right) is the permission of Sokaku Takeda for Ueshiba to teach Daito Ryu Aikijutsu, providing he takes only people of good character as students. It also states that Ueshiba will forward a 'joining' fee of three Yen for each new student, to his teacher.

Minoru Hirai in 1942 at the Japan Butokukai, the central authority for martial arts at the time.

What is sure is that prior to the war he was still teaching the combat effective techniques that had been passed on to him by Sokaku Takeda. Training at his dojo was so tough that it became known as the 'jigoku dojo' or hell training hall. Injuries, frequently serious ones were commonplace, and only the very toughest survived. His most able students from this period were Gozo Shioda, Kenji Tomiki, Minoru Hirai, and Minoru Mochizuki.* Gozo Shioda seems to be the best of the students of Morihei Ueshiba that has stayed true to the original teachings of Sokaku Takeda. The very effective methods his Yoshinkan school bear witness to this, as does his involvement with training police and military personnel.

During the early part of the war Morihei Ueshiba continued to teach, but in 1942 he moved to the town of Iwama in Ibaragi prefecture and took up farming. The reason for this is unclear. One of his biographers states that this was a protest against the power of the military and the suffering that the war was causing. He might have also have felt that moving to the country was a prudent step as the religious movement with which he was closely associated, had come under the official scrutiny of the Kempei Tai.* In fact it is rumoured that the explosion that wrecked the headquarters of the Omoto Kyo Shinto sect led by Onisaburo Deguchi, was the work of the military, a reprisal for the public criticism Deguchi had heaped upon their heads.

After the war Ueshiba returned to Tokyo and calling his art now 'aikido' starting teaching again at the dojo in the Wakamatsu area of Tokyo close to Shinjuku. Older now, and motivated more and more by his religious beliefs, he changed the emphasis of his school from martial arts training to improvement of the individual through Aikido. In effect what was prior to the war a hard but effective method of fighting that taught both attack and defence, now became a religious philosophy involving the performance of the modified Aikijujutsu methods that formed the aikido repertoire.

In the years that followed Japan's defeat, with its once proud military machine now disgraced and dismantled, the words of peace uttered by

**Minoru Mochizuki introduced Aikido, Judo and Katori Shinto Ryu Iaido into Europe after the second world war and was awarded the order of cultural merit by France for his efforts.*

**The Kempei Tai were a military police unit that performed the same function, and enjoyed the same degree of notoriety as the Gestapo did in occupied Europe.*

such a charismatic figure fell upon fertile ground. Approved by the US Army of occupation as a desirable 'non-martial' pastime, Ueshiba Aikido as it is often known, prospered and out shone totally the other schools of Aikijujutsu that had been opened by other former students of Sokaku Takeda. Before long, in the eyes of the world, Morihei Ueshiba was Aikido. The art personified in the form of a venerable old gentleman with whispy white beard and sparkling eyes.

There is no doubt that Morihei Ueshiba had a powerful personality that allowed him to influence his fellow man, and created a love for him in others that caused them to suffer hardship for him on a grand scale, and enjoy doing so. Whether the power he had came from the strength of his religious beliefs, or whether it was a God given gift that he was born with, we will never know. It is sufficient to say that it was used benevolently, and many benefited from it.

However just as night follows day, every positive influence also has a negative effect, and so it was with aikido. While the Ueshiba method may have created better 'persons' because of the emphasis on character building and spiritual values, many of the techniques of the school deteriorated to such an extent that they became impractical. Many would only now work if the 'opponent' co-operated by allowing himself to be thrown. Others depended upon the opponent actually participating in the performance of the technique by taking a firm hold on the defender by which he could be thrown.

What Morihei Ueshiba could do as a result of his extensive knowledge of Takeda (Daito) Ryu Aikijujutsu and super human personality, others could only emulate by performing what amounts to a stylished ritualistic technique that would probably not work in actual combat, and that would sometimes require the co-operation of the victim in his own downfall. This is not a criticism, Morihei Ueshiba regarded his art as a way to God, not a method for overcoming other mortals. I have no doubt that he would be pleased to go down in history as the man that converted a martial art into a way of peace though the eternal harmony of his own method.

"O Sensei" Ueshiba died in 1969 at the same age, and within a few days of the anniversary of the death of his own teacher Sokaku Takeda. What he left was a group of very dedicated students, devoted to him and determined to carry on the work he had begun. His son Kisshomaru Ueshiba became the second headmaster of the school, and the fame of the method continued to spread. But for many, the school was the man and no one could replace him. When his light was extinguished it was to his followers, almost as if an eclipse of the sun occurred that punctuated history for a brief instant, before the light fell again upon the ground beneath.

Morihei Ueshiba demonstrating the striking techniques of Daito Ryu Aikijujutsu.

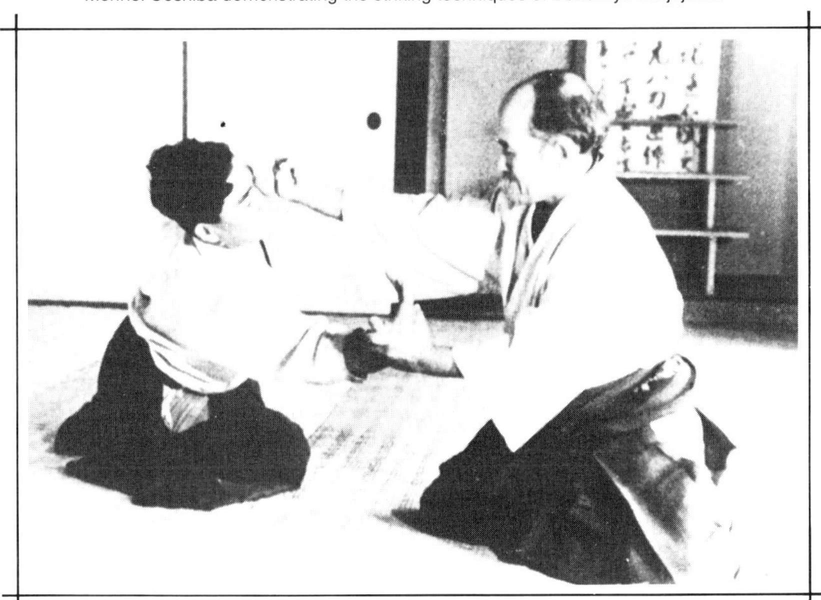

6 Gozo Shioda and the Yoshinkan

Right: Gozo Shioda, a student of Morihei Ueshiba for many years before the last war when the latter was teaching Daito Ryu Aikijutsu. At this time Ueshiba taught in a similar manner to his own teacher Sokaku Takeda, and as a result his school was known as the 'jigoku', or hell dojo. The change to the 'soft' style 'aikido' did not take place until after the war. Gozo Shioda still teaches the combat effective methods he learnt during the pre-war period, through his own Yoshinkan Aikido organisation.

Born the son of a wealthy and influential doctor, Gozo Shioda developed an interest in the martial arts early, and it was an interest that has lasted his lifetime. His father, as was the practice at that time, had many apprentices and assistants who lived in his house and studied under him, as well as helping out with general tasks. To prevent idleness when they were not working or studying, and to keep them in good physical condition, Dr. Shioda established a Judo dojo in the house where the young men were encouraged to train.

As well as studying judo in his father's training hall which was called the "Yoshinkan", young Gozo also developed an interest in Kendo. However, it was his desire to test his skill at judo that led him to the dojo of Morihei Ueshiba, a teacher of Daito Ryu Aikibujutsu, and a former senior student of Sokaku Takeda. His judo was so ineffective against the techniques of Aikibujutsu, that on May 23rd 1932 at the age of 17 he became a member of what was known as the "jigoku" or hell dojo. Morihei Ueshiba was at this time 49 years old and at the peak of his ability.

Shioda was a student at Takushoku University, an institution that continues to produce outstanding martial artists to this day. He was one of the "three tough guys" of Takushoku, the others, Masatoshi Nakayama who would go on to become the chief instructor of the Japan Karate Association and Masahiko Kimura, for many years the all Japan Judo Champion. Shioda graduated in April 1941 and at the age of 26 was sent to China to make his contribution to the war effort. His teacher Morihei Ueshiba was at this time teaching at the Rikugun Nakano Gakko, an intelligence academy for high level army officers, as well as the Rikugun Toyama Gakko that taught amongst other things the deadly Toyama form of swordsmanship (see "Naked Blade" and "Crimson Steel" by the same author).

In 1946 when hostilities ceased, Shioda returned to Japan and resumed his studies with Master Ueshiba, only to leave some time later to start his own movement which he named "Yoshinkan" after the judo dojo of his father. Master Ueshiba, by this time in his sixties was gradually changing his martial art into a spiritual movement, while Shioda, now the founder of his own movement and therefore known by the title of 'Kancho', preferred to maintain the original and combat effective methods that he had learnt before the war. Thereafter, the Yoshinkan would be noted for the toughness and skill of its members, and the effectiveness of their techniques. As a result, they remain to this day the preferred school of the police and military.

In July 1954, in an All Japan Martial Arts Exhibition Gozo Shioda was given the highest award of all the one hundred groups participating, which greatly enhanced the reputation of the "Yoshinkan", and helped to establish it on a firm footing. This was a turning point for the Yoshinkan, and confirmation if it was needed, that Gozo Shioda intended to follow the old ways of the Daito Ryu tradition and not deviate from them, or accept any compromises in the way they were taught or performed. Representing Morihei Ueshiba's group at this demonstration was Koichi Tohei.

Gozo Shioda has many stories to tell of his days as an apprentice to Morihei Ueshiba. Space would not allow us to even include a tiny percentage of them, so we have chosen one which not only gives an insight into the character of Morihei Ueshiba, but also very graphically demonstrates the difference between martial arts and sports. Sporting events after all are held at a pre-determined time and place, so the competing athletes can bring themselves to a peak of mental and physical ability at the correct time. Martial arts skill however needs to be available twenty four hours a day, regardless of the physical and mental condition of the exponent, the location in which he finds himself or anything else for that matter.

At the request of Admiral Isamu Takeshita, Morihei Ueshiba agreed to give a demonstration of aikido before the Japanese royal family. Prior to the demonstration, Ueshiba was very ill with jaundice and could barely eat or drink, and was so weak he could not walk unaided. On the day of the demonstration he needed help to dress and so bad was his condition that the two students he had chosen to assist him, Shioda and Yukawa were sure he could not go on with the 'enbu' or demonstration.

However, as the introduction was given and the audience began to applaud, Master Ueshiba went through a transformation. His eyes began to sparkle and his posture changed completely Gozo Shioda recounts, it was if he had recovered from the jaundice in a few seconds. As the demonstration began, Yukawa went to great lengths to compensate for his teacher's poor condition, and as a result was injured. Failing to get up from a powerful throw, he was found to have broken his arm and was not able to continue. This left Gozo Shioda to act as Master Ueshiba's assistant for a non-stop forty minute demonstration of throws locks and holds. As a result of the punishment he received, following the demonstration he ran a dangerously high fever for a week. The lesson is clear, mastery of the martial arts opens the door to mastery of both the body and mind.

Below: The 'aiki-nage' of Yoshinkan Aikido.

Gozo Shioda has frequently been chosen to demonstrate before figures of international importance such as the Japanese Royal Family, Princess Alexandra of Britain and Robert Kennedy of the United States. Kennedy was introduced to Gozo Shioda by Yasuhiro Nakasone who would later become the Prime Minister of Japan. During his visit to the Yoshinkan, Kennedy explained to Shioda how dedicated, tough and well trained his bodyguards were. He proudly stated that they were neither surprised by, nor frightened of anything and invited Shioda to try them out. One of the very heavily built bodyguards suddenly grabbed Shioda who is only five feet tall and weighs 110 pounds, and pushed him. Without hesitation or conscious thought of any kind, Shioda applied the 'yonkajyo' technique and effortlessly forced the huge bodyguard to the floor and on to his stomach.

Kennedy was much amused by this, and jokingly suggested that he should dismiss his secret service bodyguards and hire members of the Yoshinkan to protect him instead. In a book that he subsequently wrote, Kennedy mentions this incident and recounts that the bodyguard said that he did not eat breakfast that morning. Whether this was meant to be the reason for his failure to subdue a man half his size we will never know, it remains an amusing incident that clearly demonstrates that even against highly trained, physically superior antagonists, correctly applied techniques still have the desired effect.

Gozo Shioda is rightly regarded as one of the foremost masters of Aikido in the world today, and one of the few who can claim to teach the old, combat effective methods of aikijujutsu. It is interesting to note how history repeats itself in the progress of ancient aikijujutsu into the twentieth century. Nearly all the senior masters have been small men. Sokaku Takeda and Shiro Saigo both stood about five feet tall and weighed in the region of 110 lb, as does Gozo Shioda. Morihei Ueshiba was a little taller and about 40 lb heavier.

Also, all of them studied from their teachers when the teacher was in his prime. For example, Morihei Ueshiba studied under Sokaku Takeda from the time his teacher was fifty five years old until he reached sixty two. Gozo Shioda studied with Morihei Ueshiba from 1932 when Ueshiba was forty nine, until the war interrupted his studies nine years later. This repetition of technique being passed on to selected students at a particular point in a teacher's life when his physical and mental powers are at their peak, must be regarded as significant if only for the fact that all the greatest teachers, generation after generation, have acquired their technique in this manner.

Below: 'Shiho-nage' performed by Yoshinkan founder, Gozo Shioda.

Gozo Shioda and the Yoshinkan occupy a prominent place in the Japanese martial arts community, but are not so well known as yet to the outside world. The author is in fact a long time "uchi-deshi" or live-in student of Gozo Shioda, and continues to pass on the knowledge that he acquired when he was a member of the elite Yoshinkan professional instructors group.

7 Analysis of Aikido Movement

I chose 'Shiho-Nage' to demonstrate aikijujutsu movement because as it evolved directly from 'yoroi kacchu kumiuchi' or grappling method for the armoured warrior, I felt that it might be easier to understand in this context. For example, a Samurai who had lost his sword in battle, would not try a last desperate attack on his still armed opponent by striking his protective armour (for obvious reasons). Nor by throwing himself at his legs in a rugby type tackle (thereby exposing his neck to a fatal cut or thrust). Rather, as can be seen from the wood block print opposite the contents page of this volume, he would grasp his opponent's arms to prevent him using his sword and by controlling his wrists, attempt to throw him to the ground with 'shiho-nage', literally four directions throw.

Whether it is used to deal with an unarmed opponent, or one armed with a knife or sword, the essential movements of the technique are the same. You avoid the initial attack by correct timing, then using your opponent's own force and adding your power to it you employ the resultant energy to overcome him. This is the theoretical concept of course, in fact timing, correct movement and the effective application of a painful wrist lock are all necessary components of a successful throw. As a large amount of pain is generated when the lock is correctly applied, shiho-nage is useful when dealing with an opponent who is larger, heavier and/or stronger than yourself.

Shiho-nage can be used to counter any type of assault. Strikes from the front or side, grabbing attacks etc. can all be overcome with this versatile and very effective technique, or by one of its derivatives such as Shiho-nage Kuzushi (where the opponent is thrown to the front or side), of which there are many variations. A word of caution is necessary however. As shiho-nage involves throwing your opponent to the floor on his back, it is difficult for all but the most experienced to perform a sucessful ukemi, and injury can therefore result if care is not exercised. Train but train safely!

SHIHO NAGE

Although its name implies that it is a technique that can be performed in any of four different directions (shi = four; ho = direction; nage = throw) it can actually be used in any direction and its flexibility is almost unlimited. It is an extremely effective throw in which the opponent is thrown forcibly to the floor backwards. Caution must be exercised in practice therefore to prevent unnecessary injuries.

A variation is Shiho Nage Kuzushi in which the opponent is thrown to the front or side with an outside or inside turn.

Shiho Nage is a combat effective technique that comes down to us from antiquity. As it was developed for use on the battle field by armoured Samurai, the movements should be performed in a vigorous manner, and not as if they were dance steps. Speed, power and accuracy are necessary for the successful performance of this technique.

1. You are faced with an armed opponent who is obviously going to attack you with his knife.

2. As he strikes, pivot on the right foot, swinging the left foot to the rear, as you block the attacking arm with your left hand. The block, coupled with the strike to his face will cause him to lose his balance.

3. At this point you can harness your opponent's power, and add your own to it as you grasp his wrist and start to swing it up in front of you.

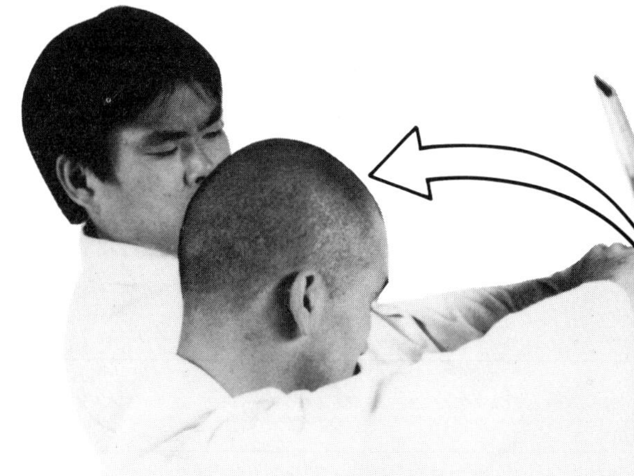

4. Slide the left foot forward along a straight line, and raise your opponent's hand as if you were raising a sword ready to cut.

Continue raising his arms, then sting on the balls of your feet, his arm over your left shoulder start to force it downwards.

6. As you continue to push his arm down, twist his wrist and start to move your weight forward.

7. Throw your opponent by pushing forward and downwards, your knee slightly bent. In a combat situation, pull a little as you throw him so that he lands badly and injures himself.

YAMA ARASHI

Literally 'mountain storm' this technique did in fact fall into disuse with the advent of modern Judo and was 'lost'. However our research reveals that it must have been performed as shown in this section. 'Yama Arashi' was made famous by Shiro Saigo when he was fighting for the reputation of Kodokan Judo, against the older schools of Jujutsu. No Judo man since him has been able to perform this throw, and it seems that it was never included in the curriculum of the Kodokan.

To perform 'yama-arashi', as you grapple with your opponent, block or slip inside his arm, crouch and throw him in one fast movement. Variations include using your leg to help with the throw, throwing the opponent onto his head instead of away from you and a greater degree of emphasis on a wrist hold to perform the technique.

1. As you grapple with an opponent, take hold of his collar and right arm.

2. Holding him firmly, step to the side with your right foot to break his hold . . .

3 . . . then stepping in under your opponent's arms, apply pressure to his neck and twist his arm. Then as your hip touches his body . . .

4 . . . applying still more pressure to his neck through the hold you have on his collar, lift him at the point that your hip touches him . . .

5 . . . and in one continuous movement, throw him forward and down by shifting your weight forward and pulling down with both hands.

SANKAJO

This technique which was developed from the short sword technique, is especially useful for the smaller person when faced with a large opponent, and clearly demonstrates the effectiveness of Aikijujutsu.

Whatever type of attack is launched against you from the front or rear, take hold of the aggressor's arm and concentrating your power into it, throw him or apply the lock as you slip under his arm. This technique is very useful as a method of performing an 'arrest' without causing injury to the 'suspect'.

NB. The first five movements of Sankajo as we have shown it here are the preliminaries to two different conclusions, the throw that occurs in movement six and the alternative restraining technique, movements seven to ten. In other words, the principal can when he reaches movement five, either throw his opponent or restrain him.

1 . Facing your opponent in a left stance, he adopts a right stance.

2 . Step forward and to the left, grabbing his right hand and striking him strongly in the face.

3 . While he is momentarily stunned by the blow, step in under his arm and take hold with your right hand as well . . .

4 . . . apply pressure to the wrist, twisting it so that your opponent's fingers point towards his own ribs.

Apply more pressure to raise your opponent he tips of his toes, thereby unbalancing him.

6 . . . then holding the wrist lock firm, step forward with the right foot while pushing down your hands and throw him.

7 . Stepping back with the left foot, pull and twist the opponent's wrist clockwise and take hold of his elbow with your right hand.

8 . Continue to step back, applying yet more pressure to the wrist and elbow.

9 . Then by pivoting on your left foot, force him to his knees by applying still more pressure to his arm and wrist.

10 . Force him down all the way to the floor then take complete control of him by putting your left leg against his arm and pushing down on his elbow.

KOSHINAGE

Koshinage involves, as the name implies, a technique in which you throw your opponent across your hips, 'koshi'. More precisely, you divert your opponent's power to unbalance him, then stepping in with your leg between his you lift him onto your hips and throw him down. It is essential that at all times you keep firm hold of the opponent and do not allow the lock to loosen on his arm or elbow.

The key to the successful application of 'koshi-nage' is the control and balance of your ankle, knee, hip and upper body. Variations include foot sweeps and hooking movements to facilitate the technique and make it stronger.

1 . You face a knife wielding assailant, both of you in left stance.

2 . As he cuts at the side of your head, step forward and slightly to the side, raising your arms as you do so . . .

3 . . . then pivot on your right foot to avoid the cut as you simultaneously block the knife hand and strike your opponent in the face.

4 . Step to the right as you take hold of the opponent's wrists . . .

5 . . . and twisting the wrist to the right and stepping forward at the same time . . .

6 . . . step in under his arm so his elbow is on your shoulder, and shifting your weight to the left foot and making contact with your left hip against his body . . .

7 . . . in one continuous movement, pull a lift your opponent over your back . . .

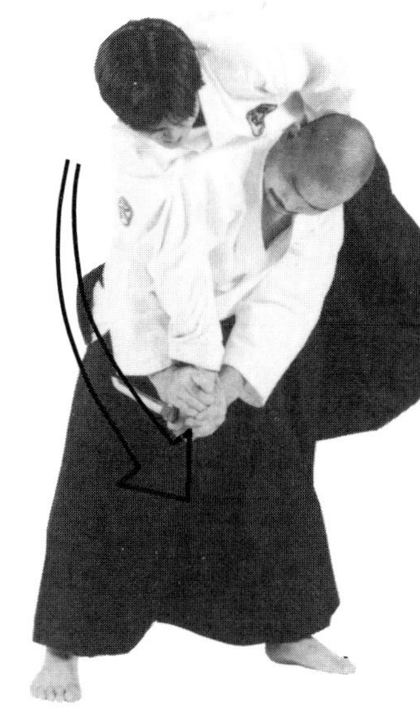

8 . . . and throw him by dropping your right shoulder and raising your left as you pull your arms down.

IRIMINAGE

Is a difficult but very effective technique that takes many years of practice to master. It is based upon the principle of stepping in diagonally to meet an opponent's attack so as to break his balance and throw him. If this stepping movement is to the front it is called 'jitsu' a diversion, if to the rear it is termed 'kyo' a feint. There are many variations within this basic concept.

Irimi nage is a very important technique which depends for its success on understanding the opponent's intentions and timing. This is why it takes so long to polish to a standard where it can be used effectively in actual combat situations.

1 . In this application or irimi-nage, you are facing an opponent armed with a sword.

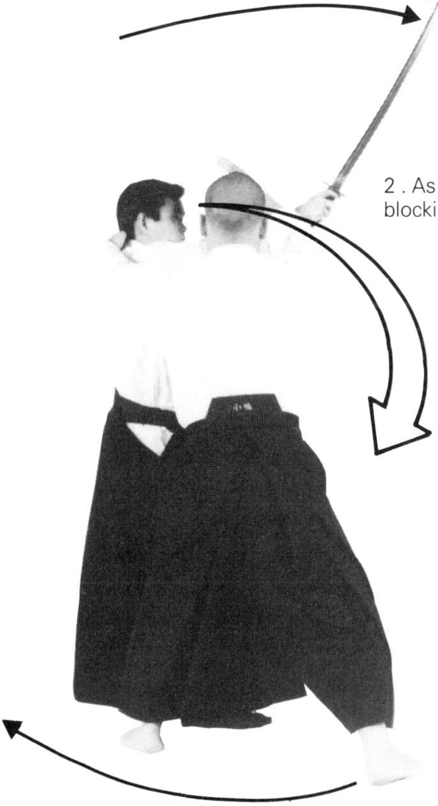

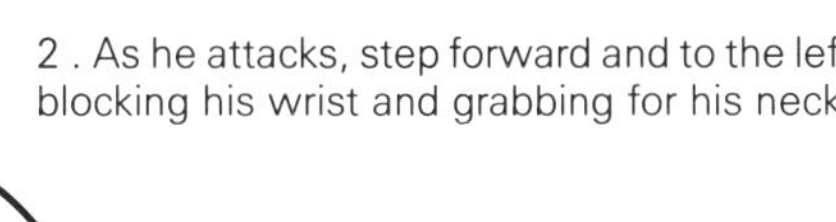

2 . As he attacks, step forward and to the left blocking his wrist and grabbing for his neck.

3. Pivoting on your left foot, control his hands with your right while grasping his collar from behind.

4. Shift your weight to your right foot as you take his hands downwards.

5 . Shift your weight back to the left foot and bring your right arm up under his chin while you control him with your left hand . . .

6 . . . then step forward with your foot as you push forward on his neck to throw him to the floor.

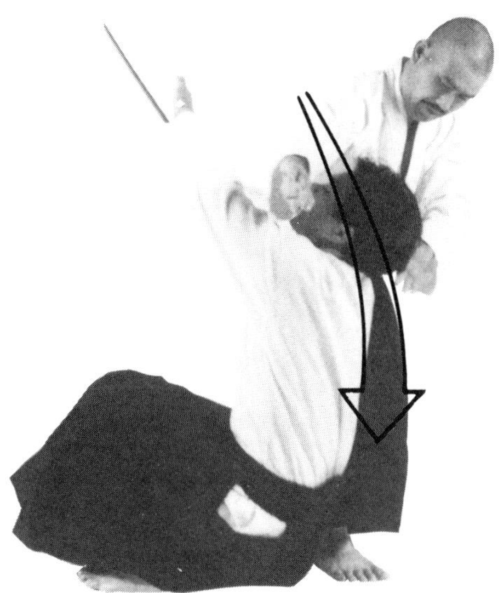

TACHIDORI KOTEGAESHI

When your opponent launches his attack, step into his blind spot with an evasive movement 'irimi'. Then taking hold of him, guide his sword, and therefore his body to your balance point (that is the point at which he loses his balance), and twisting his wrists with extreme power, throw him down. This technique can also be used to subdue the opponent once thrown and allow you to safely deprive him of his weapon.

1. You are facing an opponent armed with a sword.

2. As he cuts at you, step forward and slightly to the left to block his wrists . . .

3 . . . then pivoting back on the left foot, slide your left hand down until your thumb rests on the back of your opponent's right hand . . .

4 . . . and with your right hand supporting your left thumb, twist your opponent's hands anti-clockwise as you step back with the left foot.

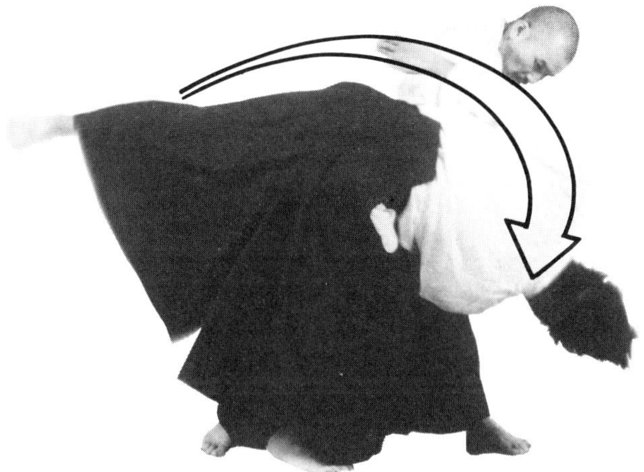

5 . Continue twisting his hands while twisting your hips in the same direction . . .

6 . . . to throw him to the floor . . .

7 . . . keeping control of his hands and therefore his weapon throughout the movement.

KOTE GAESHI DORI

Is an effective technique when dealing with a physically larger or armed opponent, as it allows you to keep your distance without sacrificing effectiveness. It is performed by grasping the opponent's wrist and forcing it outwards in order to throw him to the ground.

1 . You are facing a menacing opponent.

2 . As he launches his attack, step diagonally forward to left . . .

3 . . . to block with your left arm, then sliding it over his right . . .

4 . . . continue sliding your left hand down until you can grasp his hand, and twisting it anti-clockwise . . .

5 . . . continue to apply pressure to the wrist to control him as you strike him strongly on the chin.

6 . While he is stunned, force his right arm down to the side . . .

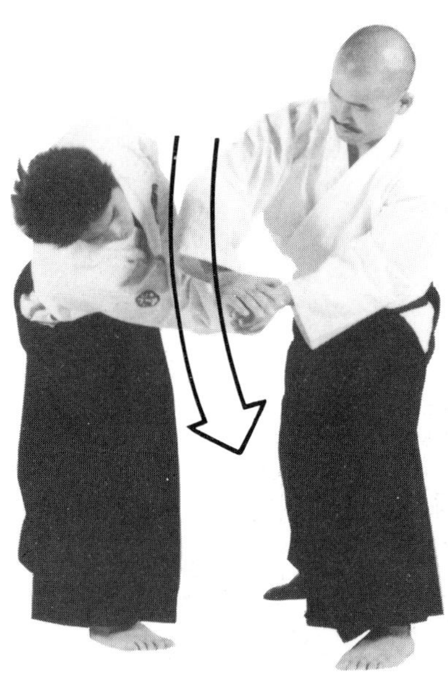

7 . . . then throw him by forcing down hard with both hands and shifting your weight to your left foot.

8 . Keep hold of your opponent when he lands on the floor . . .

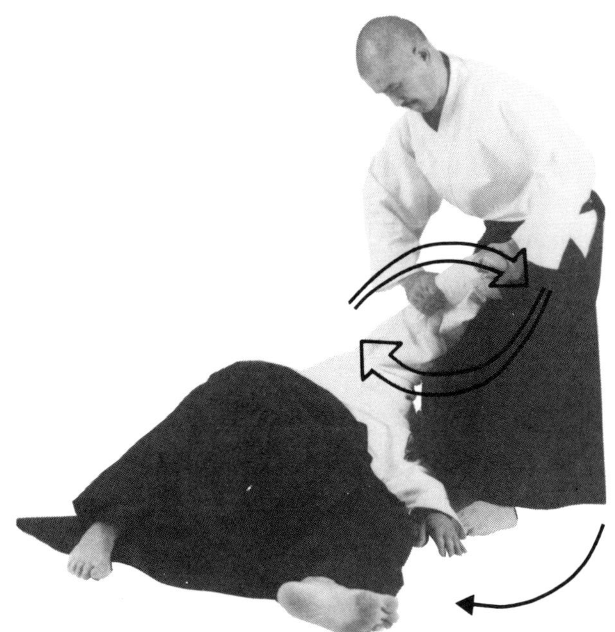

9 . . . step forward with the right foot and taking hold of his elbow with your right hand and twisting his wrist clockwise with your left . . .

10 . . . continue the twisting motion to force him onto his face.

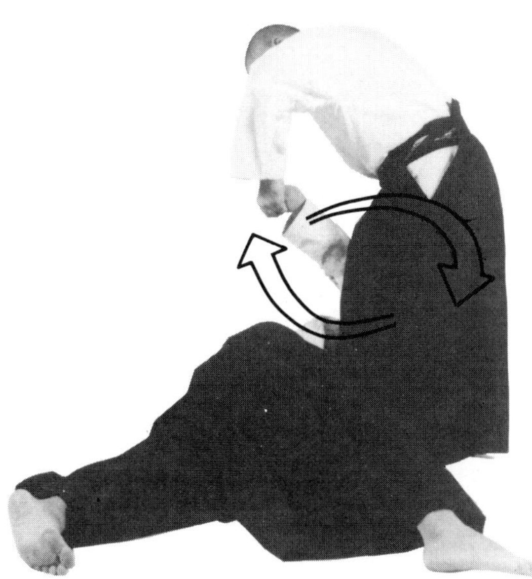

11 . To complete the control hold, apply pressure to his shoulder by holding his right hand securely in your left, his elbow on your right and bending at the knees.

YUBIDORI

The fingers, 'yubi' are one of the weakest parts of the human anatomy, and therefore convenient for the application of great pain in order to subdue and/or control a violent and aggressive opponent. The three techniques that follow are ideal in a self-defence type situation, and also for law enforcement officers who require techniques that maximise effect while minimising the risk of serious injury.

Whether the lock is applied inwards from the outside or outwards from below, the most effective control can usually be exercised by grasping two of the opponent's fingers. One finger breaks easily, three offer a lesser degree of control, especially if your opponent is a trained martial arts person, and if you take hold of four fingers, a strong opponent could resist you.

1. You are facing an opponent who offers you his hand.

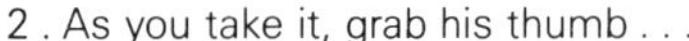

2. As you take it, grab his thumb . . .

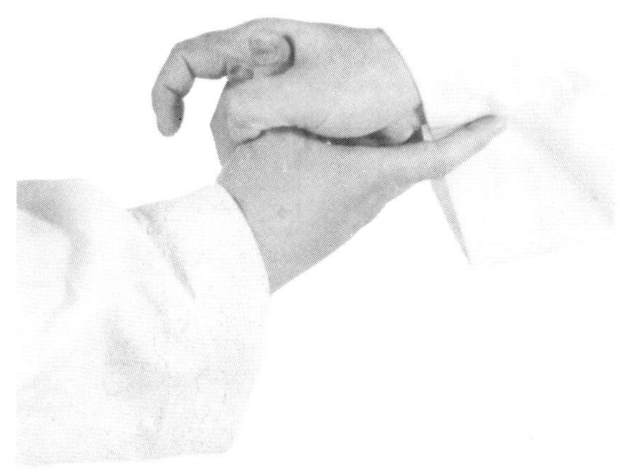

Close up of the grip.

3 . . . and apply pressure to it.

4 . Moving your hands to the right, break your opponent's thumb by striking it with your left hand, . . .

5 . . . then twist your right hand back to unbalance him and prepare him for a throw.

1. Grab your opponent's index, middle and ring fingers . . .

2 . . . then step forward and twist his wrist clockwise . . .

3 . . . until his palm is facing you, whereupon you can force him onto his toes and break his balance by applying even more pressure.

1 . Grab the top of your opponent's fingers with your left hand.

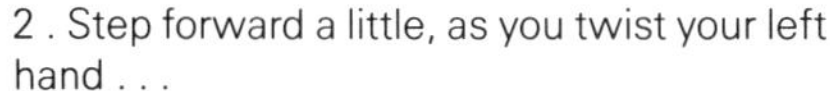

2 . Step forward a little, as you twist your left hand . . .

3 . Push in with the right hand at the wrist . . .

4 . . . so you can apply a forceful lock to your opponent's wrist.

NIKAJO

This technique is effective against grabbing type attacks directed at your arm sleeve, shoulder or chest. It involves locking the opponent's wrist into an 'L' shape then pulling downwards to apply pain and therefore control. It can be applied by swinging your hands down as if cutting with a sword, or by pressing against your attacker's wrist as he grabs at you, and increasing the power of the technique by reinforcing it with your shoulder. This latter variation causes a ten-fold increase in pain and is therefore very effective.

1. Grab the top of your opponent's fist with your right hand.

2. Grab his wrist with your left hand and twist in a clockwise direction . . .

3 . . . until his fingers point straight up, when you can push down on his wrist to force him to the floor.

SANKAJO DORI

Sankajo dori is a technique that has stood the test of time and from its Samurai aikijujutsu origins has passed into the self defence arsenal of knowledgeable law enforcement officers in many countries, as well as Japan. It is easy to learn and apply, and allows even a small person to take complete control of a larger opponent and place him in a prone position (for handcuffing), or subdue him in a safe manner until help arrives.

1 . Grab your opponent's left hand with your right, and twisting it anti-clockwise . . .

2 . . . move in under his arm, striking his with your elbow as you do so.

3 . Grasping his hand with both of your own, shift your weight back on to your foot to complete the lock.

4 . Continue twisting his arm to unbalance him . . .

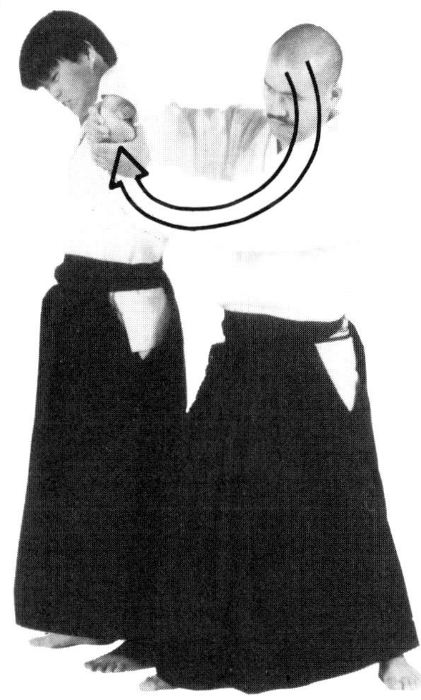

5 . . . then bringing his left hand behind his back . . .

6 . . . grasp his elbow with your left hand and his wrist with your right, as you apply an arm lock.

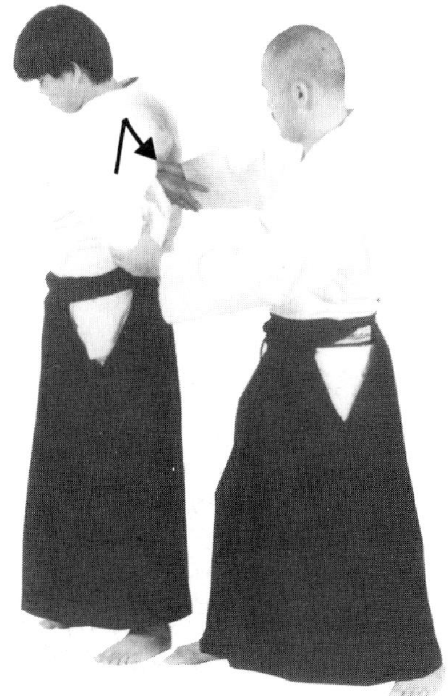

7 . Using your opponent's elbow as the pivoting point, bring his wrist forward without at any time losing contact . . .

8 . . . then force his wrist down to unbalance him.

YONKAJO

This technique is a difficult one to master and depends on the application of power to a weak point on the inside or outside of the opponent's wrist. Many beginners make the mistake of using simply grasping power rather than the whole force of the body channelled through the hands, and therefore find it difficult if not impossible to apply effectively. To the experienced performer, it is a useful technique for applying in a crowded place and one that can have a powerful effect on an opponent.

Sokaku Takeda demonstrated this when he applied it to the wrist of the hapless Mr. Perry, who had asked for him to be ejected from the train in which they were both travelling. It was also used by Gozo Shioda when he effortlessly demolished Robert Kennedy's huge secret service bodyguard.

1 . Grab your opponent's wrist with your right hand, and his fist with your left.

2 . Then applying upward pressure with the base of your right index finger, force his wrist upwards keeping it in line with your left hand.

3 . Then direct the pressure from the base of your index finger in a downward direction . . .

4 . . . continuing until your opponent is on the floor.

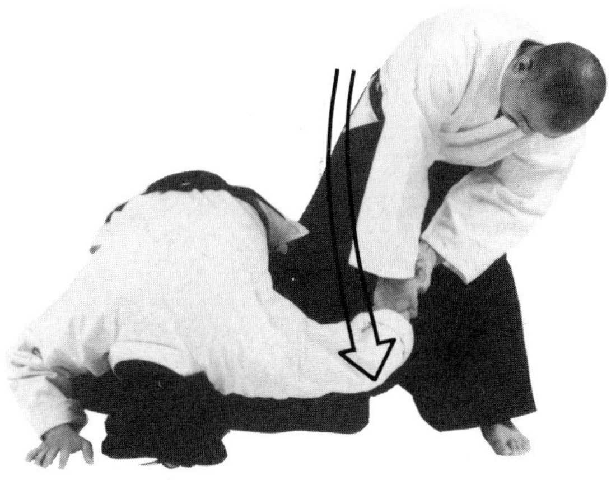

KOTEGAESHI MAKI

This technique involves twisting the opponent's hand outwards in order to make him lose his balance and take control of him. Against an experienced martial artist, or a person of great physical strength it is difficult to apply effectively in its basic form. In this case, by placing your arm under his, extra leverage can be obtained that will allow you to subdue even a very strong opponent.

1 . Grab your opponent's right hand with your left . . .

2 . . . and twisting it anti-clockwise . . .

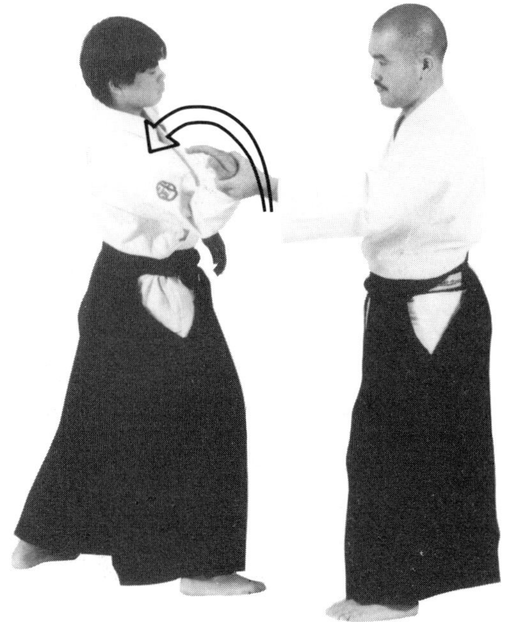

3 . . . bring your right arm through to reinforce the hold . . .

4 . . . and push down to subdue him.

Close up of movement 4.

KOTE HINERI

When your opponent tries to grab your hand, you brush his away then taking hold of it you twist it strongly. Timing and correct body turning are important if this technique is to succeed, as is the need to accurately judge your opponent's intentions. This is true to a greater or lesser degree of all such techniques.

1 . You have grasped your opponent's hand.

2 . Step to the side with the right foot twisting your wrist anti-clockwise as you do so.

3 . Continue twisting until the back of your hand touches your left hip . . .

4 . . . then add your left hand to the grip, pivoting on your left foot as you do so.

5 . Using the power of your hips and your hands, continue twisting until your opponent is forced to the floor.

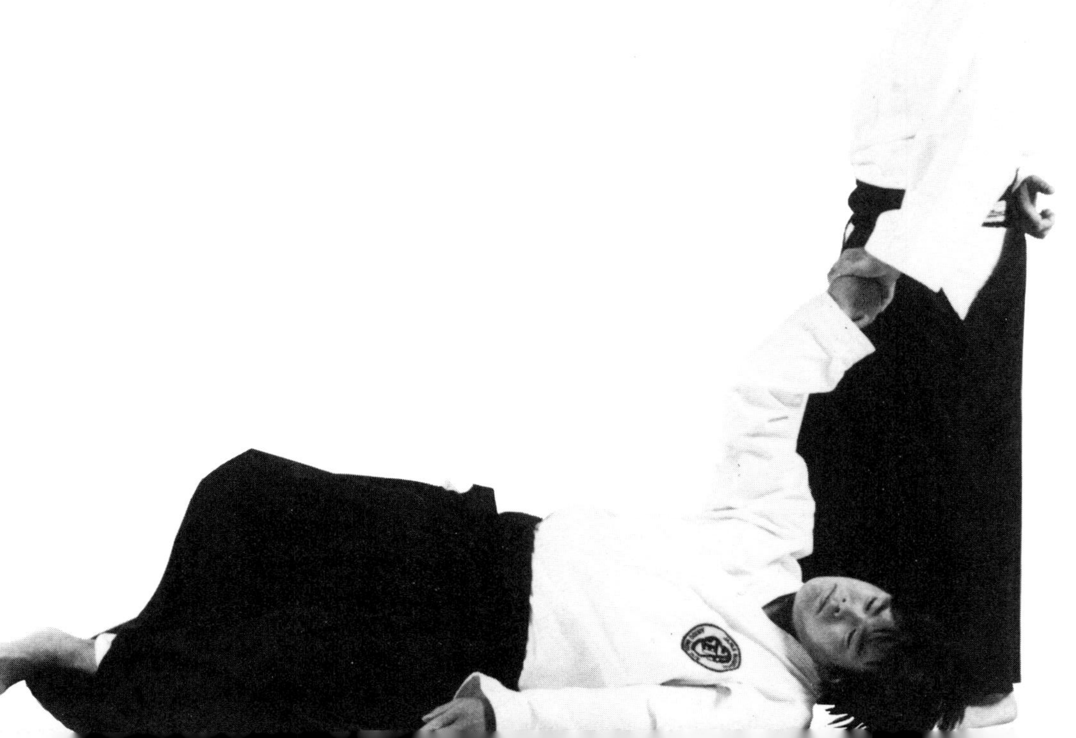

HIJI DORI

Most aikijujutsu techniques involve the locking of joints in the direction that they normally bend. Hiji dori however, is applied by locking the elbow joint in the opposite direction either from underneath or outside, while concentrating all your power into it.

Needless to say, it is a very effective technique that can break the elbow even before the opponent is thrown, and is a fundamental technique in weapons control. Effective body swerving 'irimi', technique and timing are important for the successful application of hiji-dori.

1 . Grasp your opponent's hand and twist it anti-clockwise.

2 . Still twisting his hand, step forward with your left foot as you place your left arm over his right . . .

3 . . . and winding your arm around his, take hold of your own right wrist . . .

4 . . . and twisting your hip forward, put pressure on his elbow to unbalance him.

Close up of movement 4.

HIJI KIME

This is a variation of Hiji Ate involving the application of an elbow lock in the standing position followed by the opponent being thrown backwards or forced down onto his face and subdued. In the case of the opponent being thrown backwards, the lock is applied from the inside. When the control hold is applied, the elbow is locked from the outside. This is a popular technique that has found its way into martial arts other than aikijujutsu.

1 . Take hold of your opponent's right hand, and twisting it anti-clockwise . . .

2 . . . reach forward and grasp his collar.

3. Then stepping forward with the left foot, pull down on the right arm to unbalance him . . .

4 . . . then pull down sharply to bring him under control.

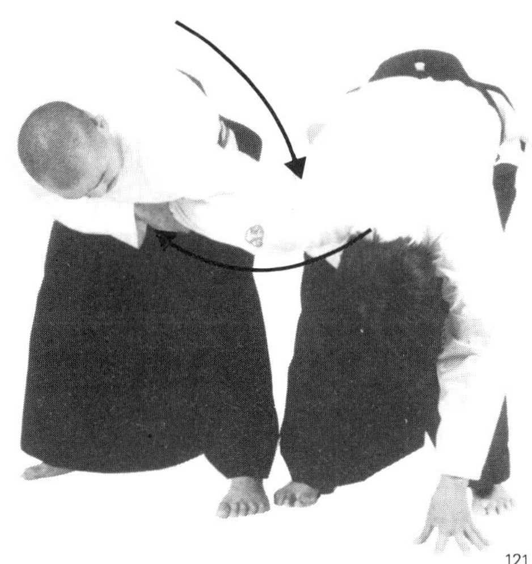

ANCIENT TECHNIQUES

In feudal times the correct method of seating oneself, especially when in the presence of superiors, was in the 'seiza' fashion with toes tucked beneath the body, back straight and the bottom resting on the soles of the feet. The Samurai, being professional fighters, quickly developed methods of dealing with acts of violence when seated in such a manner that were effective, yet allowed them to restrain transgressors without rising to their feet and thus insulting their Lord. Long swords were not allowed indoors and thus attacks, when they were made, usually involved a knife or short sword. Aikijujutsu techniques were only taught to the highest level Samurai and this gave them an advantage over the lower level retainers which they jealously guarded. The very skilled Samurai could restrain an armed man without causing him injury, and this degree of technical excellence was very much admired.

IKKAJO

Two Samurai are seated facing their Lord when an argument starts and one reaches for his short sword. As he commits himself to the attack, the would-be victim blocks his sword arm and applying pressure to the elbow, subdues him and forces him to submit. It is important to get close to the attacker on the outside of his arm, so that you can control him even if he pushes forwards or pulls back.

1 . Both you and your opponent are seated in the formal fashion.

2 . From the corner of your eye you see him reach for his weapon . . .

3 . . . and as he cuts at you, you move forward with your left leg, blocking his elbow with your left hand and his wrist with your right.

4 . Applying pressure to the elbow, and twisting his wrist strongly in a clockwise direction . . .

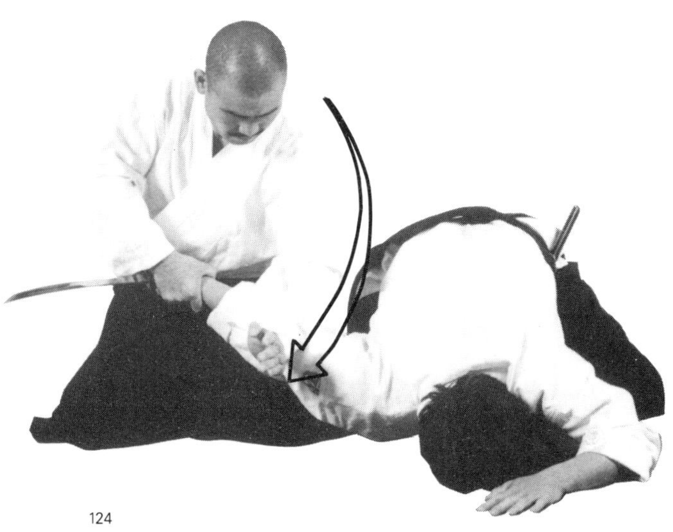

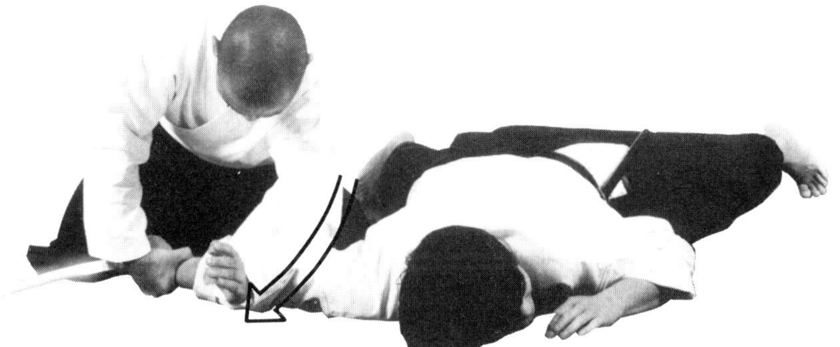

5 . . . disarm him by forcing his elbow to the floor and pulling his wrist up against it.

NIKAJO

This technique is very useful when defending from a seated position, as the most likely attack you will face is a thrusting one, rather than a cutting one. As the attack is made, the body is moved out of the path of the knife and the opponent's wrist captured. Then turning back, his wrist is forced downwards in a motion similar to that used to cut with a sword, and the attacker subdued.

1. You and your opponent are seated, when you notice that he . . .

2 . . . is reaching for his weapon.

3 . As he draws, turn, raising your right knee as you do so . . .

4 . . . then as he thrusts at you, pivot back to avoid the blade and grab his right hand with your right.

5 . Pivot back to face him, bringing your left hand to join your right as you twist his wrist clockwise.

6 . Move forward on your left knee until your opponent's arm is under your own, twisting his wrist all the time, until you can disarm him.

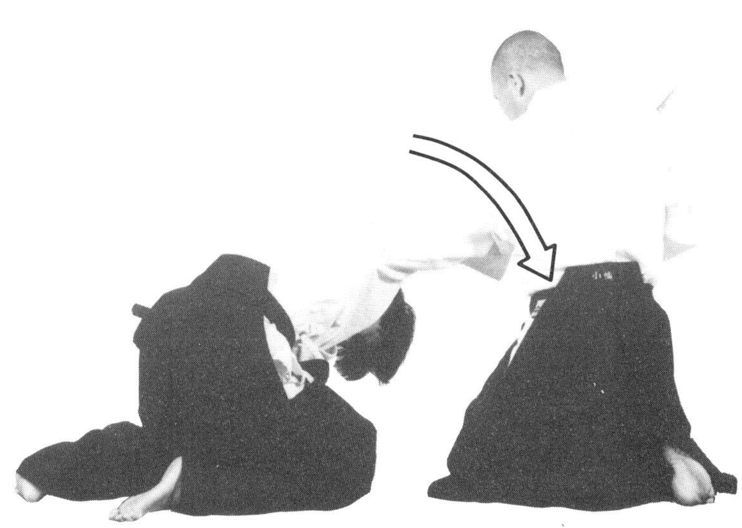

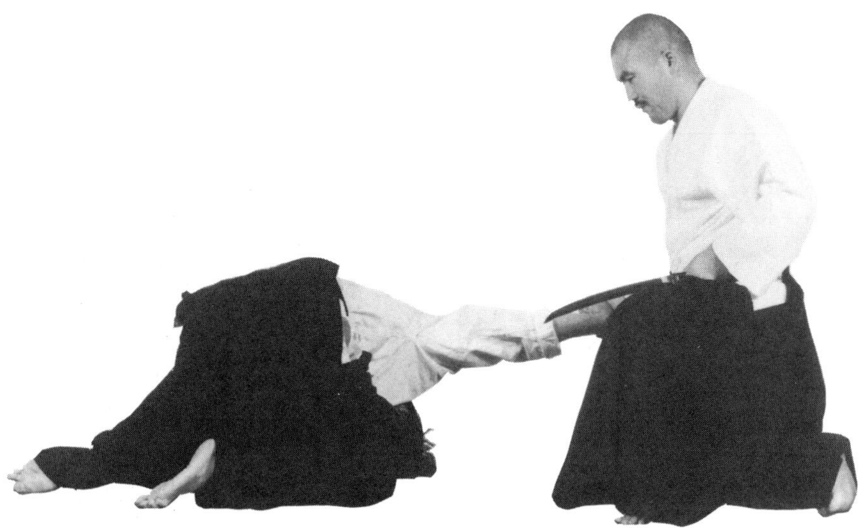

7 . Maintaining your grip and therefore your control over him, disarm your opponent.

KOTE OSAE

During the feudal era the formal salutation was a seated bow, performed by placing the left hand on the floor followed by the right, then including the body forwards. The left hand was placed on the floor first so as to minimise the time the right hand was away from the weapon in the waistband. Generally speaking, the left hand would be used to block an attack, while the right drew and retaliated with the short sword or knife. In this instance the right hand is used to block and grasp the attacker's hand prior to the lock being applied.

1. You are seated opposite your opponent in the formal manner.

2. Your opponent reaches across in an attempt to grab your short sword . . .

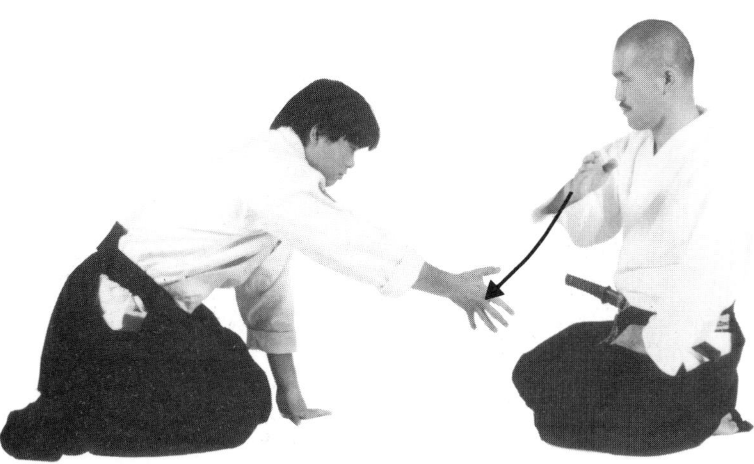

3 . . . as he closes in on you, move slightly forward and to the side blocking his hand as you do so.

4 . Without losing contact with his hand, take firm hold of it and grabbing his collar with your left hand . . .

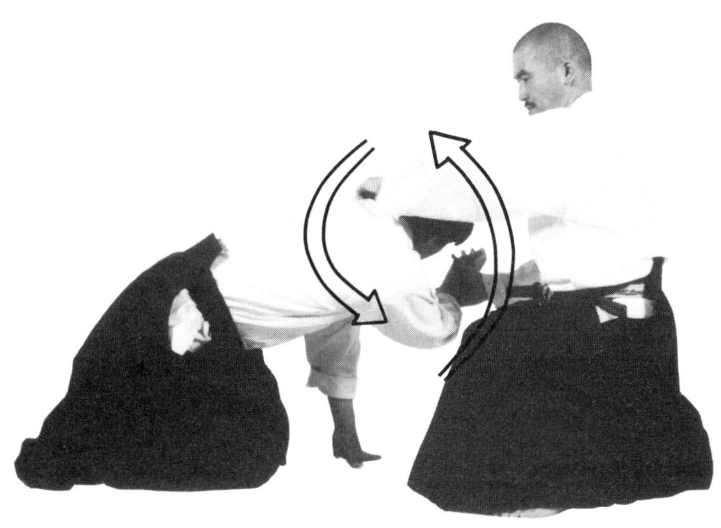

5 . . . force him to the floor by pivoting backwards on the right knee, and twisting your arms anti-clockwise as you do so.

6 . Move forward controlling your opponent by taking hold of his wrist with both hands and pushing forward on it.

HIJIATE

Yagyu Munenori, the sword instructor to the second and third Tokugawa Shoguns, developed a number of effective 'mutodori' techniques for use by unarmed Samurai facing an armed opponent. It should be noted however that the unarmed combatant is at a severe disadvantage, and for this reason these techniques were only effective if he was considerably more skilled in the fighting arts than his assailant. In this example, 'higi-ate' is used in conjunction with the 'mutodori' principle to defeat an attacker armed with a long sword. From this it would be clear that the action takes place outdoors, as only short swords were worn inside the house.

1. You are facing an armed opponent.

2. As he moves forward and launches his attack, you step in to meet him with your left foot, blocking his wrist with your right arm, and elbow with your left hand.

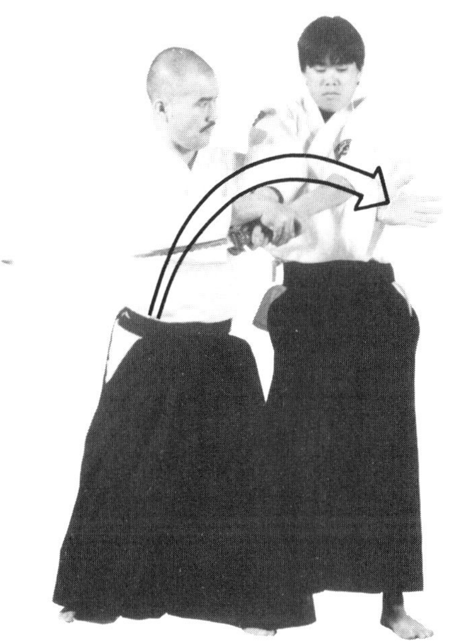

3. Pivot on your left foot, controlling his hands with your right, as you place your left arm under his right elbow.

4. Push down with your right hand to put pressure on his arms and unbalance him . . .

5 . . . and keeping hold of his weapon, throw and disarm him at the same time by stepping forward with the left leg and pushing forward on his arms.

ASHI DORI

This technique was developed for close quarters use on the battlefield between fully armoured warriors. It exploits the fact that a Samurai equipped in this way, would have great difficulty rising to his feet once he had been thrown on his back. The technique is applied after a feint to the head, and is both painful and very effective.

1 . You are facing an unarmed opponent.

2 . Move into the attack with your right foot, and grab him by his shoulder and wrist.

3 . Then put the arch of your foot against the heel of his right foot, and leaning forward on his shin bone, push him down.

4 . Maintain control of your opponent by putting your weight on his shin.

9 Conclusion

As I said at the beginning of this book, we must study the old to understand the new, and this is especially true of aikido. We must study the methods of Sokaku Takeda, why and how they were changed by his students especially Morihei Ueshiba, and what effect the changes had. If we do not do this, if we blindly follow where others lead without research, we will never know if what we practice is effective or not. Aikido has changed greatly in the past eighty years, we must take care that we do not allow it to change too much so that it becomes simply a shadow of its former self.

The techniques of Daito Ryu Aikijujutsu were passed from Sokaku Takeda to Morihei Ueshiba when both were at an ideal age. Sokaku Takeda was at the peak of his ability; his student was young, tough and in possession of a tremendous thirst for knowledge. The importance of this cannot be over-estimated as this is how the true techniques of any martial school has been passed on to ensure its survival. From the best teacher at the prime of his life, to the youngest, toughest student.

Let me explain it this way. The rocks in the upper part of a stream are rough and unpolished like the character and technique of a young teacher. Where the stream reaches the ocean, even the largest and strongest rocks have been reduced to small, smooth pebbles. Half way between the source of the stream and the ocean, the rocks in the stream are large but smooth like a martial arts teacher in his prime. This is as true in life as it is in aikido, I urge you to seek out the best teacher you can so that you can learn from him when he is at the very pinnacle of his ability. When strong and effective technique is tempered by stability of character, consideration and experience.

The second point I would like to make concerns the tendency we all have to be self centred and narrow minded. Many modern martial arts are very easy to overcome because they are practised in isolation, and become weak and effete as a result. The 'ryu' of the Samurai were composite arts that endowed the fighting man with many different disciplines. The knowledge he acquired of a whole variety of weapons, ensured that his techniques were kept combat effective. The modern enthusiast however tends to practice one martial art only, and as a result does not understand what he would be likely to face in actual combat, or how he could deal with it. Aikido against aikido breeds weakness and self deceipt.

As a professional swordsman I can assure you that modern aikido could not deal with the repeated attacks of an expert swordsman. Aikijutsu or more correctly aikibujutsu could, and did because the insight given by a deep understanding of swordsmanship, would allow an unarmed Samurai to defend himself effectively. I strongly recommend any serious aikido enthusiast to study swordsmanship, tanto-jutsu and other weapons. A knowledge of these will not only greatly enhance your technique and its effectiveness, but allow you to enter an entirely new and exhalted level of expertise.

I sometimes visit aikido demonstrations as a spectator and I am ashamed at the antics of some instructors. Do they really expect people to believe that three able bodied swordsman can be rooted to the spot by the power of 'ki', or that an opponent can be thrown twenty feet across the floor by a poorly executed technique? Do they believe it themselves? This profanity angers me greatly and is an insult to the memory of Sokaku Takeda and Morihei Ueshiba. Of course 'ki' is important, but so is timing, skill and strength. There are many factors in the aikido equation and 'ki' is not the most important one.

We must go back to the time just before the last war when both Sokaku Takeda and Morihei Ueshiba were active, and study the techniques that they were both teaching. Before he grew old, Ueshiba was known as an extremely vigorous teacher, and serious injuries at the 'jigoku' dojo were quite common. We should resist with all our energy, the understandable desire to copy the techniques of a teacher in his advanced years who had lost his vigour, no matter how well loved and respected he may be. To slavishly copy the technique of one's aged teacher is not to show him respect, but to mock him. Research rather the techniques of his golden years if you wish to build a living monument to him.

We have lost sight of the roots of the arts that we study. For the Samurai there were major (dai-no-budo) and minor (sho-no-budo) martial arts. The major arts were for use on the battlefield and included, swordsmanship, the use of the spear, strategy etc. and the minor arts augmented them, jujutsu for example, and were used when a warrior found himself unarmed. They existed successfully together and were taught as one system. Once separated, both lost a great deal of their potential, although obviously the major arms involving weapons, still prevailed over the minor, unarmed ones.

Strong aikido cannot exist in isolation. As a minor martial arts it should ideally be supplemented by a major art such as the sword, so that a well rounded student is produced who can meet and face an armed opponent and overcome him. All martial arts have their strong and weak points, and we must understand them honestly and make allowances for them. The weakest point of a human being is ignorance.

I also resist most strongly the teachings of many instructors who say that power should not be used in aikido, stating that Morihei Ueshiba expounded this theory. In his golden age, Ueshiba was feared for his vigorous execution of Daito Ryu techniques. His teacher Sokaku Takeda, spent twenty years travelling Japan challenging and beating the greatest masters of all martial arts. People who avoid hard and powerful techniques will never pass to the upper levels of aiki knowledge, they will remain trapped forever in the purgatory of self-satisfied ignorance that besets so may of today's aikido students.

If two antagonists have equal ability, the stronger one will win. If one has great power but is deficient in technique, the one with more ability may be able to overcome him. These are facts not theories. If you are told that 'ki' will overcome both strength and technique, do not believe it, you are being deceived. I want everybody to understand real aikido, I am not a critic but a proponent who wants to promote the art in the best way possible.

To avoid facing up to the truth, some may question my right to speak on this subject in the hope that the points I have made may be ignored, and things proceed as they have done before. I am happy to give you something of my experience in the martial arts which starts at the age of eighteen with a six year period as an 'uchi-deshi' of Gozo Shioda. I went on to study swordsmanship under Taizaburo Nakamura, Nobuharu Yagyu and Tesshinsai Uchida, as well as a variety of weapon arts from Motokatsu Inoue. As proof of the practicality of my technique I can offer two examples, not as a way of boasting about my own ability, but simply to illustrate the effectiveness of the techniques that I have been taught.

When I was living in Tokyo I prevented the murder of a neighbour who was being strangled by an intruder, and as a result received a commendation from the Chief of the Metropolitan Police. More recently I was attacked in Central Los Angeles close to the civic centre, by a knife wielding assailant, and disarmed him and held him for one hour until the police arrived. This is the sort of aikido I would like to see practiced, not the type whose effectiveness can justifiably be questioned even by members of the public, with little or no knowledge of the martial arts.

Around 1580 Yamamoto Kansuke* wrote the book 'Heiho Okugi Sho' (the inner secrets of martial strategy). This manual was for use by the Takeda Samurai from whom our present aikido techniques were

**Yamamoto Kansuke was the premier military strategist of the Takeda clan at this time, and helped develop a battlefield strategy that so impressed Tokugawa Ieyasu (who was a victim of it on one occasion), that on his becoming Shogun, he adopted it in its entirety as the military method of his own Tokugawa government.*

handed down, and was an important work that outlined both practical fighting methods and the principles of strategy.

These are the words of the author written four hundred years ago:

"We can separate Samurai teachers of strategy (heiho) into three separate classes.

A 'Heiho-Sha' is a Samurai who has studied deeply from many masters and added the results of his own research to his fighting method. This allows him to be ever-victorious; a virtuoso in the art of war.

A 'Heiho-Jin' is a person who has not studied the martial arts so deeply, but has picked up some good points and specialised in certain techniques which he applies at an opportune time so as to win (he picks the right time to fight). He will sometimes, but not always win.

A Heiho-Tsukai copies only the example of his master and passes on the techniques as he himself learned them, without adding his own experience. As a result the techniques decline as time passes."

I hope that you will have the ambition and the drive to climb to the heights of the "heiho-sha", to soar with the eagles and not graze with the sheep. Aikido should not be allowed to stray away from what is practical and effective, the art of war should be nutured even in times of peace.

Qui desiderat pacem, praeparet bellum
Let him who desires peace, prepare for war.

Toshishiro Obata January 1988

Bibliography

KYOYOJIN NO NIPPONSHI
published by Kyoyo Bunko.

NIPPON KASSEN ZENSHU
by Kuwata Tadachika published by Akita Shoten.

KIZOKU TO BUSHI NO OKORI
by Wakamori Taro published by Shu Ei Sha.

NIPPON BUDO JITEN
by Kasama Yoshihiko published by Kashiwa Shobu.

HIROKU NIPPON JUDO
by Kudo Raisuke published by Tokyo Supotsu Shinbun Sha.

HIDEN NIPPON JUJUTSU
published by Shinjinbutsu Oraisha.

AIKIDO KAISO UESHIBA MORIHEI DEN
by Ueshiba Kisshomaru published by Kodansha.

ZOKU UMEBOSHI TO NIPPONTO
by Higuchi Kiyoyuki published by Shodensha.

RIKAI SHIYASUI NIPPON SHI
by Yamamoto Shiro published by Buneido.

HEIHO OKUGI SHO
by Yamamoto Kansuke published by Dragon Books.

QUEER THINGS ABOUT JAPAN
by Douglas Sladen published by Anthony Treherne & Co.

THE COMPLETE KANO JIU-JITSU
by Hancock & Higashi published by Dover Books.

dragon books
OTHER TITLES

Other Titles published by Dragon Books

Nunchaku Dynamic Training
BY HIROKAZU KANAZAWA 8TH DAN
Former three time All Japan Karate Champion, and supreme master of the Shotokan style of karate, the author is also a recognised weapons expert, specialising in nunchaku and sai. His book has been acclaimed as the best produced, and easiest to understand on the subject, and takes the reader right from the most basic movements, up to a complex and dynamic 106 move kata, that develops technique and style, as well as providing a dazzling exhibition of skill for demonstration purposes. An in depth work that includes sections on history, origins, author's biography, health aspects etc. 160 pages (9" x 6") laminated full colour cover. **$9.95**

Shotokan Advanced Kata Series
BY KEINOSUKE ENOEDA 8TH DAN
Nicknamed the "Shotokan Tiger" by the students and instructors of the prestigious JKA Instructors Institute, this explosive and powerful teacher, who is noted for his practical fighting ability, must surely be the best possible person to present this important series of books. A perfectionist in all he does, the author shows by means of individually hand printed and prepared photographs, and detailed captions, every single movement of these intricate exercises with a degree of clarity never before achieved. A series that should find its way into the collection of every martial artist.

Vol 1 Bassai Dai:Kanku Dai:Jion:Empi:Hangetsu
8" x 12" 140 pages **$14.95**
Vol 2 Bassai Sho:Bassai Dai:Jiin:Gankaku:Sochin
8" x 12" 111 pages **$14.95**
Vol 3 Tekki-Nidan:Tekki-Sandan (2 versions):Nijushiho:
Gojushiho-Dai:Gojushiho-Sho
8" x 12" 111 pages **£14.95**

Shadow of the Ninja
BY KATSUMI TODA
The extensive martial arts and historical knowledge of the author, gives an authenticity and depth to this stirring tale of the Samurai Kuroda and the Ninja of the Tomokatsu clan, that will hold the reader spellbound throughout this beautifully produced book. A fast moving tale of treachery, sudden death and martial excellence in 17th century Japan, made all the more fascinating by original illustrations of Ninja weaponry and techniques. Nine sell-out editions in 25 months proves our claim that "Shadow of the Ninja" sets a new standard for books of this type in quality of production, design and content. 8" x 5" 127 pages **$7.95**

Revenge of the Shogun's Ninja
BY KATSUMI TODA
In this sequel to the best selling novel "Shadow of the Ninja" the feud between the Tomokatsu Ninja Clan and the Kuroda Samurai family, moves on a generation as it approaches its dramatic and bloodthirsty conclusion. The secrets of the Ninja are pitted against the supernatural powers of the masters of the spirit of the wind, as the Tomokatsu clan seek out the ghostly green warriors of the forests of Kyushu, for a final dramatic confrontation. An action packed story, full of accurate and intriguing information and lavishly illustrated with line drawings of Ninja techniques and equipment. 8" x 5" 107 pages **$7.95**

Ninja Death Vow
BY KATSUMI TODA
As sales of "Shadow of the Ninja" and "Revenge of the Shogun's Ninja" continue to soar, martial arts historian Katsumi Toda, presents the third part of the saga of the Tomokatsu Ninja and their enemies, the Kuroda Samurai. Set against the background of the U.S. Navy's incursion into Japanese waters just over a century ago to break down the barriers of isolation that had existed since 1600, it is a fast moving tale of revenge and treachery. When the Americans threaten to return at a later date and complete their mission, forces who wish to maintain the old system, let loose the power of Ninjutsu to aid their cause, and death and destruction stalk the land. Toda's fast moving style make the reader feel part of the story; just a page or two into the first chapter, and one can imagine standing on the deck of Commodore Mathew Perry's ship "Mississippi" as the Stars and Stripes fly for the first time over the Japanese waters of Uraga Bay. 144 pages $8\frac{1}{2}$" x $5\frac{1}{2}$"
$7.95 (available from November 1985)

The Ninja Star – Art of Shurikenjutsu
BY KATSUMI TODA
Noted Japanese martial arts historian, Katsumi Toda, reveals for the first time the results of his research into the art of star and spike throwing, as practised by the Ninja of medieval Japan. A complete work on this fascinating subject, the book includes; historical background, the development of Ninjutsu, types of shuriken and shaken, stances and grips, throwing techniques, targets, breathing exercises, kata and much more. Lavishly illustrated with attractive line drawings, it is a factual historical work, as well as a practical, down to earth "how to do it" book, and will therefore appeal to martial arts enthusiasts of all ages, styles and affiliations. 79 pages 9" x 6" full colour laminated cover, more than 110 illustrations.
$6.95

Kubotan Keychain – Instrument of Attitude Adjustment
BY TAKAYUKI KUBOTA 8TH DAN
Known to millions as a result of his frequent screen and television appearances, Takayuki Kubota, is a karate master and law-enforcement instructor of exeptional ability, who for two decades has coached the LAPD and other agencies at the highest level. His invention of the "Kubotan" a small plastic baton, (later converted to a keychain) for use by female police officers, revolutionised self-defence in the 70's, and the "Kubotan" itself has become recognised with the passage of time, as probably the most effective, legal self defense aid available to the citizen. In this detailed manual, its inventor shows a wide variety of methods for using the "Kubotan" in almost every imaginable situation. Detailed, high definition photographs and easy to understand text, allow the reader to quickly and fully understand the fine detail of how, and to what parts of the body, the Kubotan can be applied, in order to subdue even the unruliest agressor. Complete with striking points diagrams, grappling and striking techniques as well as a large selection of the very latest "Kubotan" techniques, the book represents the 'state of the art' in this field. Includes an introduction by Hollywood actor James Caan, 9" x 6" 104 pages full colour laminated cover
$7.95

Other Titles published by Dragon Books

Dynamic Kicking Method
BY MASAFUMI SHIOMITSU 7TH DAN
There have been so many books on the subject of Karate's kicking techniques, that it is difficult to imagine one that would stand out against the background of boring and often repetitive books currently available. Due to a combination of author ability, excellent design and high quality photography, this one not only stands out, it shines! Author Shiomitsu is an absolute master of the karate kick, not just a talented dilettante, the techniques that he demonstrates and teaches are the original techniques of karate, before they were diluted and packaged for the western market place and are therefore, uncompromisingly tough and brutally effective, rather than athletic or as has been happening of late, theatrical. In this detailed text he not only teaches and demonstrates these techniques, but also includes information on how training and teaching techniques have changed as a result of the efforts to 'sanitize' karate in order to make it an acceptable sport, rather than an effective means of self defence, as well as stories of karate masters who made one or other of these deadly techniques their speciality. Within the covers of this book, is a wealth of information that it would take a lifetime of training to discover. Kicks to cause discomfort, pain, serious injury or worse, depending on the circumstances, and the way that they must be practised to be perfected. These techniques, and his performance of them, have earned the author an awesome reputation, as a particularly hard and dangerous fighter. This encyclopedic work can only endorse the reputation he has acquired as a result of his many victories in and out of the arena over the years. 9″ x 6″ 132 pages colour cover **$9.95**

Balisong – Iron Butterfly
BY CACOY "BOY" HERNANDEZ
We must warn the reader that this is not an instructional book in the normal sense of the word. The techniques showing the Balisong expert Cacoy Hernandez, were developed for, and can only be used in violent circumstances; they have no spiritual value whatsoever. Cacoy ("Boy" to his few friends), Hernandez, is a fighter of the old school, rather than one of the 'actors' that currently seem to dominate the martial arts scene. Born into poverty, raised in deprivation and matured against a background of criminality, he was forced to adopt survival methods, which, although shunned by modern urban society, have allowed him to enjoy six decades, and walk away from countless confrontations. Signor Hernandez has one unshakable belief, which can be summed up by the phrase "Never reject a challenge, and never step back." This book combining as it does his Balisong technique, together with accounts of incidents in his life when he has been forced to use it, must without doubt be of interest to all martial artists. 9″ x 6″ full colour cover, 107 pages **$7.95**

Naked Blade – A Manual of Samurai Swordmanship
BY TOSHISHIRO OBATA 7TH DAN
Long hidden from the gaze of all but the chosen few the ferocious techniques of swordsmanship as taught by the "Rikugun Toyama Gakko" are revealed for the first time in the English language in this comprehensive and well produced book. Author Toshishiro Obata, is an imposing and highly skilled exponent of this sword method of the former Japanese Imperial Army. The art that he demonstrates, was so feared in the West during the last global conflict that a military training manual published at the time was prompted to advise American officers to "Shoot the officers [with swords] first" as a matter of urgency when confronting the enemy for the first time. The strength, resolve and power of the Samurai lives through the techniques that they developed; they can find no finer repository than in the skill of the author and between the pages of this fascinating training manual. 6″ x 9″ 132 pages **$9.95**

Ninja Training Manual – A Treasury of Techniques
BY YUKISHIRO SANADA
Through an unbroken chain of many generations of Ninja Warriors that stretches back through the centuries of warfare, violence and treachery to the very roots of Japanese history come the original and authentic secrets of the Ninjutsu, many being presented here in written form for the first time. **$9.95**

Ninja Sword – Art of Silent Kenjutsu
BY KATSUMI TODA
Besides being expert with weapons like the Kama, Shuriken, Kaginawa and Manrikigusari for which they are best known, the Ninja trained hard to make themselves invincible with the beautiful but deadly Japanese sword. Ninja Sword – Art of Silent Kenjutsu contains much material only previously available to martial arts historians, and very senior exponents of the ancient art of Ninjutsu. As such it offers the reader a fascinating glimpse of the "Kage No Gundan" Japan's army of Shadow Warriors, their methods and their way of life. **$7.95**

Dynamic Power of Karate
BY HIROKAZU KANAZAWA 8TH DAN
Dynamic Power welded to awesome technical ability have made Karate's 'Iron Man', Hirokazu Kanazawa a legend in his own lifetime and an inspiration to his tens of thousands of students worldwide. A three time All Japan Karate champion and one of Karate's original and most active pioneers of the sixties and seventies, he has for the past twenty years set his peers and those that have followed, a standard of excellence that was always virtually impossible to equal and that remains to this day, impossible to exceed. **$14.95**

Other Titles published by Dragon Books

Kama – Weapon Art of Okinawa
BY TOSHISHIRO OBATA
From the time that the warlord Hideyoshi outlawed the ownership of edged weapons by Okinawans, the techniques demonstrated in this book were kept hidden from the civil and military authorities, and taught only in complete secrecy to family members or "inner" students. Shogun Hideyoshi had good reason to respect the fighting ability of the islanders, for as author Toshishiro Obata shows, the twin sickles of Okinawa are among the most effective close combat weapons ever invented, and when wielded by an expert, almost unbeatable. 160 pages, 9" x 6" full colour laminated cover. **$9.95**

Crimson Steel – Samurai Sword Technique
BY TOSHISHIRO OBATA
The Samurai of Feudal Japan raised the art of swordsmanship to a level that has never been equalled. No effort was spared by these stalwart warriors in their quest for the ability, when armed with the fearsome two handed sword, to cleave an enemy in two with a single mighty stroke. 9" x 6" full colour laminated cover. **$9.95**

When The Going Gets Tough
BY COLONEL M. SMYTHE
Not for the faint hearted or those of a nervous disposition, the author's unique system of self-defence is simple but appallingly effective. Developed from personal experience during his active service career, it is to the urban misfit what penicillin is to the germ. 9" x 6" full colour laminated cover. **$7.95**

Forthcoming Titles

Close Encounters the Arresting Art of Taiho-Jutsu by Takayuki Kubota
Bo-Weapon Art of Okinawa by Toshishiro Obata
Ninja the Men of Iga by Shinichi Kano
Legacy of the Samurai – A Handbook for Swordsmen and Collectors by Toshishiro Obata
Shotokan Advanced Kata Vol 4 by Keinosuke Enoeda
Heiho Okugi Sho – The Inner Secrets of Martial Strategy by Yamamoto Kansuke (1550)
Jo – The Complete Art of the Japanese Short Staff by Hiroi & Yoneno
Mon – Heraldry of the Samurai by Obata & Sakai

Dragon Books are available from branches of B. Dalton Booksellers, Walden Books and all good martial arts and general bookstores. If you have difficulty obtaining any of these titles, please contact the publisher direct. Orders under $10 can be filled for the advertised price plus $1.50. For orders over $10 simply add 10% to the value of your order to cover freight and handling charges. Overseas customers, please contact us for details of export shipping costs.

U.K. Distributor: Sakura Publications P.O. Box 18, Ashtead Surrey KT21 2JD.

Dragon Books P.O. Box 6039 Thousand Oaks CA 91359 USA

Phototypeset in the United Kingdom by Concise Graphics Ltd. Hammersmith London